YOU CAN DO **BETTER** THAN THAT

JAMES HAKALA

Copyright © 2024 James Hakala

All rights reserved.

No part of this publication may be reproduced or transmitted in any form or by any means electronic or mechanical, including photocopy, recording, or any information storage and retrieval system now known or invented, without permission in writing from the publisher, except by a reviewer who wishes to quote brief passages in connection with a review written for inclusion in a magazine, newspaper, or broadcast.

Print ISBN: 979-8-35097-832-2

Printed in the United States of America

Table of Contents

Forward	1
My Younger Years	2
Active Youngsters	9
Ailments Galore	13
Music for the Soul	17
Moving Up in Society	20
Changing Schools	22
The Enticement of Sports	24
The Event	29
Devine Intervention	36
Reality	38
First Visit	42
Comprehension… I Can't Read	46
What went Wrong	50
Going Home	55
Mowing the Lawn with a MTD	61
Speech Therapy	63
Doctors Who make Outcomes	66
Hard Choices	70
First Day My Junior Year	74
Mr. Simons	77

License	80
Tim Pond	83
I Shot a Deer	86
Graduation	90
Selective Service	92
Marquette University	94
Amy-Jo's Birth	100
Imbibing the Spirits	102
Self-disciplined	105
Smith House	107
Arlene	111
Arlene's Awakening	117
The Love of My Life	124
Carbon Monoxide	130
Moving to Parsons Road	134
Snowboarding	137
Carpal Tunnel Syndrome	145
MyoPro	149
See in Your Mind's Eye	155

This book is an inspirational narrative told from my own perspective of the challenges I had to go in the course of my life. It's a book of love, hope and promise.

I was 15 when the happening occurred. Now, I'm 73. Reminiscing with a different understanding and insight into the difficulties I had to overcome.

This would be a good book to read if you've had any type of stroke or a brain trauma. It may give you inspiration and help you see what a person with my affliction has to deal with.

FORWARD

To My Sisters… Pam and Amy-Jo

My mind was normal… I could still think, reason, understand and recollect. That is the reason why coming back from this malaise was and is so difficult… to see other people physically doing what I used to do which I couldn't accomplish anymore. Jealousy is not a word for it. Hopelessness is. I was only 15…

An individual who is experiencing the complexity understands what it is all about… the person on the outside imagines or envisions or thinks they comprehend the insight and conception, but they don't have a clue!

~ ~ ~ ~ ~ ~ ~ ~ ~

MY YOUNGER YEARS

It was a normal childhood. My parents, Dawn (Weston) Hakala and Robert Hakala had 2 children, James (Jim) and Pamela (Pam), 14 months apart with Jim being the eldest and the one relating to this narrative.

As far as my parents were concerned, Pam and I had a good relationship with my parents. They were on the slight side of being strict disciplinarians but other than that… it was a supportive and a loving relationship.

My mother and father taught us right from wrong. They were devoted and understanding… the context that every child should have.

Dad worked in the woods as a logger. He drove a bulldozer and hauled trimmed logs to the staging area. From there, the logs were loaded on logging trucks and shipped to the mill to be made into dowels, paper and toothpicks no less!

I can reminisce about going with Dad to a woodyard during the weekend for a couple of hours. I was so excited and thrilled to be going with Dad. I had to follow his directions and instructions, like where to stand on the green and brown forest floor, when to give him a hand and when to hear those three important words coming from him to me, 'Good job, Jimbo!'

Once, Pam and I went along with my mother to give Dad 'salt tablets' during a heat spell one summer during the late 1950's. We couldn't find my father in the logging yard at first and I finally saw him, and I yelled, 'There he is!!' He came up to the car and he was a ball of sweat!

He was happy to see us, and we had a couple of salt tablets for him with some ice-cold water. The family talked for a couple of minutes and Dad felt it was refreshing to drink that cool, revitalizing liquid… water… and I bet it was!

My mother was a stay-at-home Mom which was common back in the 1950's. She kept the house clean, did laundry, cooked the family's meals, went on errands, she talked to the neighbors, one-on-one (not like today where we have emails, texts and whatnot), went on errands such as going to the supermarket and most importantly… took care of and watched over Pam and me. My Mom took care of our bumps and bruises, made sure we did our homework from school and taught us the qualities of beliefs and virtues.

This took place back in the 1950s and 1960's, society didn't have any of these indulgences that we have today. In the '50 – 70's, you'd drive around in vehicles to get from place to place in standard gas guzzling cars. To purchase gasoline at that time, during the 1960's, it was about $0.12 - $0.16 a gallon! The vehicle one drove was not the best on gas mileage… 8 – 12 miles per gallon! Not even a hint or a notion of electric powered vehicles, hydrogen innovation or 'chips' to propel your auto to go out and about. The television (TV) was just beginning to make an impact on our everyday lives. I couldn't wait for 5:30 PM EST to roll around every workday since 'Superman' came on the tube! Of course, it was in black & white but who cares!

We lived in a heartwarming home in a neighborhood on a dirt road called Pleasant View Avenue in a small town called Mechanic Falls, Maine.

Being a dirt road, I couldn't wait for Spring to arrive in our 4 Season chronology of weather-related events. I would walk home from school during the afternoon which was less than a ½ mile. Once I turned onto our dirt road, I would eagerly await water flowing the edge of the roadway. And if it was… Springtime was here!

I would begin making troughs for the water to flow more evenly and freely. Then, I would make dams so the water would form a pool with different eddies throughout the various dams along the roadside.

When I finally arrived home from school about a ½ hour late and I was sopping wet! My socks, shoes, the bottom of my pants and my jacket were soaked! My mother would yell, 'Were have you been?' from the living room. And once she saw me all heck broke loose. She scolded me and told me never to play in the water again! It worked for a while… but I just couldn't do nothing when I saw that cool, gentle liquid flowing down the edge of Pleasant View Avenue…

It was a neighborhood where everybody knew each other for better or worse. There would be gossip galore and the upgrade that New England Telephone offered was a 'two-party' line! Neighbors could listen in and hear what was going on, whereas you thought it was a discreet and personal conversation. That's how the scuttlebutt got spread around so fast in our closely held hamlet.

Often, you would see two or three women sitting outside in the late spring, summer, and early fall on their picnic table just talking about their future plans, the fashion of the day, and what they were going to have for supper that night. However, I noticed them playing a card game called 'Bridge' from time to time. That is an intriguing card game, and they were having so much enjoyment!

The whole town was built on one big corporation - Marcal Paper. Marcal Paper made toilet paper, paper towels, Kleenex and etcetera for the mercantile market nationwide.

Our neighborhood was about a mile from the mill.

Sometimes as we were eating breakfast before school. We would see Lew Bowman, our next-door neighbor, with a lunch pail in his hands, whistling away, walking to his place of work to begin his daily routines at the mill. It was a simple life and a good life.

I was having the time of my life! I was busy doing other things, like riding bicycles, doing chores, running, building forts, and pondering what I could do to make the refuge better… to make it additionally inconspicuous… to make stronger… to make it safer. Once in a while I would ask Dad, when he had finished supper, of course, to come and inspect my fort. It was an extremely proud moment in my life. Oh, to think… I was just a youngster!

I was a very quiet lad when I was growing up. I didn't say much, but boy, was I full of life! I can't recall this incident, but my mother had a good time telling her friends and acquaintances about the event.

My mother, my sister and I went to the dentist, Dr. Easton, in Norway ME. The reason we went to Norway ME was since my father knew him. My father grew up in the Norway-South Paris region and Dr. Easton was a good dentist.

When it came time for my appointment, I went into the dentist office, and he put his hands under my arm pits and hoisted me up onto a small platform that covered the armrests of an adult dentist chair. I was in for a cleaning, so it took about a half an hour for my appointment.

Again, I was a very quiet boy who, frankly, didn't say that much in public.

My mind must have really been spinning and I was only three years old at the time. As Mom was helping me get my jacket on to leave the dentist office in the waiting room, which was full of people… I questioned her by saying, 'Mom, how does Dad get his big ass onto that small table?' My mother couldn't believe it!

I didn't say 'peep' when I was out in public and now this?! She hurriedly tried to put my jacket on, but I didn't receive an answer from her. I was really interested in her response that I asked again, 'How does Dad get his big ass…?' By that time, she was shaking me! I didn't know what I did wrong! I started crying as she led me out of the dentist's office. Can you imagine what the people in the waiting room were thinking? Go figure…?

Around 1959, my father purchased a new bulldozer for his logging operation. New technology had it powered by diesel with a gas engine backup.

A diesel engine has a really hard time starting in cold temperatures. Thus, during the winter one could start up the gas engine and then convert it to diesel since diesel was much more economical to operate and a diesel engine had more power.

The first winter of owning this bulldozer was bitterly cold back in 1959 – 1960. Dad couldn't even get the gas engine started! Frustration was not even a word for it! Dad had the representative from W.D. Mathews Machinery Company (the business where he bought the bulldozer) come over twice to look at the bulldozer and even the rep couldn't figure out what was going on! My father received a suggestion from an old timer who said to start a wood fire underneath the engine apparatus. So, me and my father went over to the logging yard the next Sunday to do just that. It appears Dad had to dig 3 feet of snow away from the bulldozer.

Dad made a wood fire underneath the bulldozer, and he got it roaring pretty good. He got up in the operators' seat and tried to start it. It churned and churned and it churned… nothing. I never heard my father come out with foul language like he showed that day! I was standing right by the bulldozer with a stick I was using to hit snow off from different branches and such. But after he began ranting, I began walking off about 25 feet to another location. I just didn't know what to believe. I never heard such cuss words before! Anyway, the battery drained all its energy and that was it. The bulldozer still wouldn't start! It was a quiet trip on the way home.

I mentioned our dining room table looked out upon a big field at the corner of Water Street and Pleasant View Avenue. I had a passion for sports of all types. And 'the Big Field' is where we played every day! We, girls and boys, used to play baseball, softball (so the girls could have fun, too), football, and badminton. In the winter we would try with all our might to go sliding in the snow since 'the Big Field' had a very slight slope to it. We failed 95% of the time but boy that 5% made up for it!

During the winter there wasn't very much to do after school. It was frigid, slippery, windy, Artic gray and sometimes you could even hear thunder lighting in the distance during a snowstorm! We couldn't wait for the

Winter Solstice to be finished since that was the turning point when nature looked to Spring.

Nevertheless, the boys would go outside and skate, toboggan, sledding, flying saucering and build snow forts. While the girls would stay inside and play paper dolls!

As far as snow forts were concerned, we'd have a time and date set up after school to have it out… in other words a 'snowball fight'! We were all into seeing which side would win! It was either the opposing fort ran out of snowballs, or my team had a snowball so large that we would carry it over and drop it on the rival's roof (We'd like to build 'igloo forts' since they were solid and could withstand snowball attack's). thus, a cave-in!

Typically, we would have an argument over the objective on the conformation of who 'won' and who 'lost'! But still, it was exhilarating!

Another memory just came into focus. It was during 4th and 5th Grade at Elm Street School. I really couldn't do that much since you will find out later in reading. My sister, Pam, kept me in line. She was a year behind me in school. If I did anything strenuous or taxing, she would go home after school and tell my Mom all about it.

I cannot for the life of me remember his name, but we'll call him 'Mike' for repute. Mike was a bully and a tormentor as a student. He had a straight jawbone and good at playing sports. He was good at baseball, football, basketball, kickball and also… marbles! At marbles, we would make a 10" circular berm in the soil and play for the opposing team or individuals for marbles. There are so many different variations and methods of playing marbles I won't get into it. But Mike had such large bag of marbles attached to his belt…it made me jealous! He would often say to me, 'See, I almost got all your marbles 'hacklefucka" And would say to myself, 'What does 'hacklefucka' mean?' I was naïve and not familiar with terminology. I was a simple-minded young gentleman. Quite a few of the other students laughed at it but I didn't know what he was talking about. I thought it sounded immoral. In addition to playing marbles, he was also good at kickball… and so was I!

Kickball is something like softball. The only difference is you play with a ball like a soccer ball. I remember one time Mike was the pitcher… and I was the kicker. Mike pitched or rolled a fast ball to me. I kicked in such a way that the ball took off in a line drive directly to the pitcher…Mike. Mike tried to prevent the ball from hitting him but to no avail. The ball hit Mike in the head area. He started to call me names and came running towards me, but a teacher was there and broke up the upheaval before it even started.

In due course, I asked Dad when we were alone what 'hacklefucka' meant? I said, 'Mike calls me that every time I see him whether it's the hallway, at recess, in gym or wherever.' My father made a face. He sort of scrunched up his forehead and his left eye would begin twitching. He didn't say anything.

I asked him, 'Have you ever been called that before?' He said, 'Occasionally…' I said, 'What am I supposed to do?' Dad knew we were going to be moving soon to Auburn ME. So, he said, 'Just ignore it. Brush it under the rug. No matter how hard it is to get into a fight…just take no notice.' I did just that.

ACTIVE YOUNGSTERS

We would be sitting at the dining room table on a winter's night. My father would pipe up and say, 'If the weather is good this coming Sunday… we'll go skiing at Robinson's Hill in Minot ME!' Pam and I were so excited!

Sunday came and it was a brilliant, crisp, clear, but cold that day! Dad and I would load our skis on the car roof ski rack. My parents just bought Pam and I skis for Christmas from Paris Manufacturing Company which were supposed to be the best on the market. At the time they were wooden skis with metal edges for a better grip in the snow for basically making corners down the slope.

Dad had skis made in Finland. To me, at the time, the skis was about 10 feet long… but they were only about 8 ½ feet long! Dad would say, 'The longer the ski length is… the better control one has going down the hill.' They were all wood and came a point at the front of the skis. The skis had leather harnesses for your ski boots. They were old skis and Dad couldn't have been prouder to wear them!

After my father finished lacing the leather straps from the skis to his ski boots, he said, 'I'm going up the hill and pack the snow down so it will be much easier to ski down the slope.' Pam and I waited for about 30 minutes since he didn't make just one packed down area but two side by side. Pam and I struggled up the beaten path with our skis and ski poles to look around see the amazing sight of what we had to conquer. Dad said, 'After you get your ski boots buckled in your skis… bend your knees and go straight down to the bottom of the hill!'

That instruction from Dad was good enough for me!

The first-time skiing down the hill I wiped out 2 or 3 times on each individual run. But the 4th and final run, I had much improved! The rationale why it was the 4th and final time was since Pam and I were exhausted! It takes your legs in being in good condition and resilient. Concentration and application come into play, too. My legs weren't resilient, and the application needed some work. With due diligence… I got better with time.

I remember Pam and I participating in 'Ski Lessons' from Lost Valley in Auburn Maine. That really helped us a great deal and it gave us a since of hope and confidence which everyone should have in any sport, ambition or purpose he/she partakes.

When I was 15, I had a ski pass for Lost Valley Ski Park. All the hustle and bustle were ever so present at the ski area.

Everybody has different thoughts and ambitions related to their own being.

I rode on the T-Bar to the top of the mini-mountain. I stopped at the top of the hill. I was just looking the slope over, and this man stopped right beside me, and he looked like world-class skier! He said, 'You do a pretty good job skiing! I would like you to come out and try for the ski team?' I looked at him and said, 'I'll think on it but right now, I'm having the time of life!' He was the Ski Coach from Edward Little High School.

He didn't realize the health problems I had in the past 3 years … colds, sore throats, various malaises of some sort. Because of one type of illness, our doctor, Dr. Reeves, put me under strict restrictions as far as physical activity is concerned and I was kept in check by my parents. The coach didn't know that I couldn't participate in competitive and non-competitive sports. But I was having an astonishing time in this realm called life.

My mother and father always attempted to keep Pam and I active. They even taught us the 'card playing' game called 'bridge' when they didn't have anything to do that weekend.

I was about 10 years of age, and my mother got sick and tired of Pam and I went up to her and asked, 'What can I do now? Or 'I'm bored!'

My father and mother talked about it and they finally came up with a solution. My father was going to construct a Ping-Pong table. When they told Pam and I about it we said in unison, 'A Ping-Pong what?!' We had never heard of it before! My father said playing ping-pong was something like playing tennis but on a smaller scale. Ping-Pong was played on a table with the scoring principles somewhat like tennis.

Dad and I went over to Meserve's Lumber and cut two 4 1/2 x 5 sheets so it would be easy to store. Next, we took 2 large sawhorses and used them for legs. Lastly, my father and I put the net which to be quite rigid to play a good game of Ping-Pong or table tennis, which some prefer to call it.

Sometimes, after supper during the hours of the evening during the winter, Dad would ask us if we wanted to play Ping-Pong for an hour or so. We would all get excited and say, 'YES!!'

The family would go down to the cellar and have a fabulous time. All in all, Ping-Pong is excellent for your coordination, your balance and to lose weight! You really make a 'sweat' when you really get into it! We would play for hours(s) down in the cellar and we'd have so much joy and excitement!

My competitiveness was shown through when we're playing any type of sports. I was always thinking to myself what went wrong with that particular play and how I could do better and to improve on the sport in question.

I never asked Dad where he learned to play Ping-Pong. It could have been when he was in service during WW II, or it could have been when he attended Paris High School. He was an excellent player!

Growing up during this time, I had one person I wanted to emulate… Dave Wing. He was my cousin on my mother's side. He was born to Elmer and Irene (Weston) Wing. He was a fantastic and incredible athletic competitor. He could play baseball, football and basketball. And he was good at whatever sport that happened in season!

I can reminisce about being up to his home in Brewer ME. I was about 13 years old. His family lived in a split-level home and his bedroom was downstairs. Dave was doing exercises to work up for the upcoming football season. He had a bunkbed type of sleeping arrangement. He hopped up on the upper bunk and started doing sit-ups. These were not normal sit-ups… Dave had his butt on the edge of the bed and perpendicular to the length of the bed… his upper torso hanging in midair! I thought he was going to break his neck! But when he started doing sit-ups, I couldn't believe it! I said to myself, 'WOW!! I'm going to strive to be like him!'

AILMENTS GALORE

I was constantly having colds and sore throats especially during the winter. The colds were not too bad. My mother said it was because I wasn't dressed warm enough and I got too cold when playing outside. Little did she know way back then that colds were by, and still are, air-borne transmission.

Running nose, congestion, boils, cold sores and sneezing were par of the course. But when it came to sore throats, I had to be careful. Almost every time I came down with a sore throat it would lead to 'strep throat'. Strep Throats are a precursor of scarlet and rheumatic fever. Thus, one has to be careful and prudent whether you're a doctor, nurse or caretaker.

I conjecture I didn't have enough sense to tell my mother when I was coming down with a sore throat. Or I just didn't care, or I kept it secret since I was having a ball doing what I was doing. I knew I'd have to be isolated for a week or two and I didn't want that. Thus, it festered… got infected with bacteria… had a fever with the chills and bedridden!

When I was 10, I had glandular fever. Another way to express it is a 'kissing virus' or MONO. At that age I didn't have the slightest urge for girls… period! I couldn't fathom how I got it. Most likely through someone coughing or sneezing on or near me. The doctor, Dr. Ferris, ordered me to lie in bed for a month! And that was just at the beginning of school summer vacation! Darn!!!

I can remember Jeff Bowman coming over and wanting me to come and play outside. I pleaded with my mother to let me go out to the front lawn and sit. She was adamant that I was to stay inside and watch our black and white television. And I assume she got on the phone or met in person with Jeff's mother, June Bowman, and told her in an implicit way that Jeff was totally banned from our yard until further notice!

I loved baseball. Every night after supper all us guys and gals would gather in 'the field' for a game until dusk. On a clear night when the moon was full, we would play until finally one of the mothers in the neighborhood yelled, 'Billy, it's time to get ready for bed!!' Then the team broke up and the conglobation of competitors went on their merry way home.

Mr. Purington was our pitcher. Every time he pitched a ball to me I slammed it to the other end of the field! Mr. Purington had a lot of contacts in the town of Mechanic Falls. So, one day he came up to me and asked me if I would like to try out for Little League? I said, 'Sure. But first I would have to ask my parents.' I was only 7. Traditionally, they usually don't try out for Little League until you're 8 or 9 years old.

Kenny Roberts was my coach. He instructed and prepared me to play baseball like a real pro. I was 12 and I was so excited since I was going to be playing 1st String! I played short stop... the reason being, I was so fast on my feet. Someone hit a grounder at me. I went to catch it, and the ball made an odd hop just before it hit my glove. It ripped my thumbnail way back on right-side throwing hand, so it was at a 90-degree angle to my thumb!

My mother was watching us practice and when she saw the commotion over in the infield she came running over. She saw what had happened and Coach Roberts asked her if she could take me over to the doctors (Back then, society's lifestyle didn't have ERs like they have today. The ERs were aimed for automobile accidents, heart attacks and such).

She took me over to Dr. Ferris's office which was on the second floor of a restaurant in the heart of the town. The doctor's office was free of patients, so, he took me right in. The first thing he did was listen to my heart with a stethoscope. Next, he bandaged up my thumb to take care of my thumbnail. He also gave instructions to my mother to care for it. I was already to get up and leave when he said, 'Not so fast.'

Dr. Ferris put his stethoscope on my chest once more and listened to my heart for it seemed like hours! Finally, he put his stethoscope down on the table and he stared directly into my mother's eyes. He said, 'I want you to take Jim home and put him straight to bed. He is not to get up and he is supposed to lay flat. I'll be over in a couple of days to check up on him. Jim's got rheumatic fever.

Rheumatic fever is a scarring of the heart valves that an irregular heartbeat or a murmur occurs.'

My mother said, 'But Jim's bedroom is upstairs. What do I do in that scenario?' Dr. Ferris said, 'Have Bob (my dad) lift him up from the living room couch and carry him upstairs for the nighttime. In the morning, Jim can go down the stairs one at a time and go straight to the couch and spend the rest of the day in a flat, laying position.'

I thought it would be for about a week or two since that was my opinion, I felt fine… no sore throats though I did have a slight fever. This went on for about 3 (three) months!

On the way home from the doctor's office, I was really upset! I was fuming! I was contemplating baseball and my first year on the starting string in Little League. I was opining about summer vacation and going up to my Aunt Viv's camp for sometimes 2 weeks straight and having so much fun! I really was in a predicament!

About two weeks into my treatment and healing, I was introduced to a new medication called penicillin. It had fairly recently come on the pharmaceutical market, and it was considered a miracle antibiotic. One pill was as big as a Franklin half dollar! And I had to take these 3 (three) times a day! And I thought to myself, 'How am I ever going to get this down my throat!?' I ended up chewing the pill, and brother, did it taste awful! My mother ended up cutting the pill in half and then I could swallow it with no aftertaste! The penicillin pills got smaller and smaller as the weeks went on as the pharmaceutical companies got more proficient in the fabrication of the pills. What a relief!

During the month of August 1963, my father had to go to Fort Drum, New York, for two weeks. Dad was a Master Sergeant in the Army Reserves. My father was a senior technician in the motor vehicle division of a transportation brigade. Every year the army reservists had to commit to 2 weeks of training in the reserves to sharpen their skills and to learn new, upcoming technology.

Dad was also the individual responsible for taking me up the stairs every night for 3 months! I assume I was too much of a weight for my mother to do it. So, he was talking to 'Red' Meserve, our next-door neighbor, over various things, and my health came up. Dad really didn't know what he could do the 2 weeks he was at Fort Drum in the fact that he had to carry me up the steps to go to bed every night. 'Red' said, 'If you don't mind… I'll come over and take him up the stairs.'

Accordingly, every night at exactly 8:00 PM (he was in the service too and fought in World War II) 'Red' would be over to our house… exchanged a few congenialities with my mother… come in the living room… picked me up from the couch… and carried me up the stairs to my bedroom. Now if that isn't devoted commitment and dedication, I don't know what is! I was glad when Dad arrived back from Fort Drum since going to bed at exactly eight o'clock was getting to be a pain.

Once Dad got home from Fort Drum, Mom pleaded to Dr. Ferris on my behalf, if I could go outside and sit in a foldable chase. Dr. Ferris hummed and hawed. Finally, he said, 'Yes. I don't see why it would do any harm.' My heart was getting cleaner and stronger, listening to the regular 'thumps' through his stethoscope. The next day was sunny and warm. Mom set me up outside with the chase and she said, 'You're all set, and you've got several comic books and be good…' So… I sat and sat and sat and sat. I said to myself, 'This is sort of boring. There must be something else I can do.'

In conformity, I came up with the idea. There were many houseflies and mosquitos constantly landing on me outside sitting on chase. I had my mother load up a dish container with water and a little bit of dishwater soap. Every time a fly would land on me, I'd squirt it into oblivion! I believe we've actually got a voiceless video on it! That made sitting outside on the chase a little bit more enjoyable.

MUSIC FOR THE SOUL

At this point, I was an active youngster at my age! Always had to be doing something! My parents and I knew it. My parents knew I had to have some activity or extra-curricular encounter to be dedicated to. I couldn't go to the gym. I couldn't run or peddle a bike. I couldn't be active in any type of sports since of my rheumatic fever episode. The doctor's orders and my parents were so willing to follow his directives to the tee!

One late summer's night, three weeks before the start of school, we were sitting at the table after supper. My mother was talking, and she said, 'You know I think Jim ought to get interested in music'. I thought to myself, 'Music!! Music!! What an awful idea!'

Never in the world would I have ever conceived of picking up an instrument and blowing on it! But then my mother explained to me the limitations that I was up against. As I thought about it. Taking up a musical domesticated device and propelling air through it… didn't sound like too bad of a proposal.

My father tried to instill in me the trumpet. With just 3 (three) valves, I couldn't see making all those notes! I wanted an instrument that was more practical, more mellow, and easier to manage. I always enjoyed listening to Benny Goodman. He was the lead player in the 'Benny Goodman Band' (real original title for an ensemble). He played a clarinet, and the clarinet had all those keys for individual notes… how could you go wrong!

A few days later, I found out that my next-door neighbor, Carol Stone, same age as I, was also going to play the clarinet. Me, her and many others were going to comprise the Elm Street School Band! The first arrangement or musical group, the autumn of 1963, of an assemblage of musicians Mechanic Falls Maine ever had! I assume one could say Mechanic Falls Maine was progressing in this paradigm world of ours.

I was young and self-conscious. I didn't like the feeling of being with all those other kids. It just gave me an odd feeling. It made me feel secure knowing there was going to be someone in the band that I knew and could relate to.

Carol and I were eager to receive our clarinets. They arrived at Elm Street School and all the members of the band were there to receive their individual instruments. My parents and Carol's parents agreed that once we received the clarinets, I and my parents would go over to Carols house and practice on our new clarinets.

My parents, Pam, my sister, and I went over to her house just after we received our instruments. We all had quite a time in putting together our clarinets since a clarinet came in 5 pieces! The 4th and 5th sections were difficult since one had to attach them with an adjoining clasp. When we finally accomplished the feat and our reeds (a reed attached to the mouthpiece which could vibrate) were in place we began to blow our clarinets.

All I could recall is my father bringing his hands to ears attempting to impede the music in the Stone's living room! It was so loud, shrill and extremely agonizing! He and Gardner Stone, Carols father, and my father finally went outside to talk about events taking place today in our little slice of heaven. Carol and I eventually finished for the night. We disassembled our clarinets and apportioned the 5 individual pieces back in the small suitcases (cases) they came in. A propos, we didn't have our first lesson yet. Carol and I thought we did a pretty good job!

Being a clarinetist at Mechanic Falls ME was noteworthy. I played the clarinet at the Lion's Club gatherings of Mechanics Falls ME at Christie's Restaurant on several occasions.

I can reminisce our Elm Street Band Director, Mr. Edward's, was going on vacation for 2 weeks. At the end of one lesson, he asked me if I would be willing to give lessons to other clarinet instrumentalists while he was gone. I said, 'Me??' He said, 'Yes… you. You have the ability and comprehension to do a real good job!' Thus, I gave other clarinetist lessons for 2 weeks! It became quite comfortable at the end of the 2-week session. But boy… was I glad when he finally returned from his vacation.

MOVING UP IN SOCIETY

In due course, my father acquired a mail contract through the United States Post Office (USPS), July 1, 1962. He had been trying since 1958 to employ the USPS. My Dad was trying to obtain employment which guaranteed and ensured income for years to come. Transporting the US mail by an independent contractor was one of the least known employment opportunities in the United States. One had to bid on a solicitation. If you the lowest bidder at the 'close', one got the contract for several years.

And it's far better than working in the woods where you'd have to be concerned about mother nature implications, the Season's and having to pay your bills on time. True, working in the woodlands gives one a sense of freedom and no quotas to fill but working for the federal government gives one an assurance of a fail-safe income.

The whole family was happy for Dad! We all knew it would be a more comfortable life growing up under the roof he put over our heads.

As far as I was concerned, I was still under the watchful eye of Dr. Edward Reeves. The reason we had to change doctors from Dr. Ferris to Dr. Reeves was twofold. The first was we moved locations from Mechanic Falls to Auburn which was a distance of 12 miles. Back then, the doctors were local and served their community. Dr. Reeves was located in Lewiston ME… just a stone's throw off the Androscoggin River. Lewiston and Auburn way back then, were known as the Twin Cities. Second, was my father knew him. Dr. Reeves used to be his doctor when my father used to live up in the Norway – South Paris ME region.

My parents gave Dr. Reeves a monthly up-date of my activities the month prior. And if they had any questions, they could call the doctor and would either say, 'Yes or No'. No contact or non-contact sports in school. That followed through with the playing of sports in my back yard!

After Dad had the USPS contract for a year or two, a principal residence went up on the market right across from the Sectional Center where he unloaded and loaded mail for his particular route, Auburn ME – West Bethel ME. The property was located at 80 Maney Road, Auburn ME. Dad didn't have the money for a down payment or mortgage. He was just getting started on a new business venture and money was quite hard to handle on a month-to-month basis.

Thus, my grandparents, Carl and Hannah Hakala, bought the place lock, stoke and barrel! I imagine there was some sort of a Promissory Note signed, or knowing back then, (my father was the only child) Grampa and Grammy just took a good handshake with my father… and that was that!

CHANGING SCHOOLS

It was quite an adjustment changing schools. You're comfortable with your schoolmates at Elm Street School and the friends you've made in the slice of heaven you called home. This new revolution of changing erudition faculties Central School in Auburn ME was 3 to 4 times larger than Elm Street School in Mechanic Falls ME. When the students changed classes, say from English to History, it was a mile and a half you had to walk to arrive on time to your next class.

The students had gym twice a week at Central School. I had meticulous restrictions on what I could do during the 6th Grade. In the 7th Grade, Dr. Reeves let up on those limitations, somewhat. It was just that I couldn't participate in competitive sports. Thus, it gave me free reign to do basically anything as long as it wasn't compromising.

It was May 1963. The gym class was outside doing different aspects of Track. The last exploit of the day was doing a Relay Race with 5 teams competing, 4 on a team. I was to be the last one on my team to receive the bayonet. By the time I took the bayonet, my team was 4th place out of 5 and way behind. It was the distance of the perimeter of a football field that we had to run. I grabbed the wand and took off like a shot! I ran and ran and ran! I kept passing the ones in front of me! Then I could hear my physical ed instructor, Mrs. Keene, yelling, 'Run Jim… Run!!!' I finally passed Brian Lambert who was huffing and puffing and beat the whole bunch! When I finished, Mrs. Keene rushed over to me and said, 'Good job Jim! I'm proud of you!'

But music kept me going. I was in Elm Street Band and Marching Band. I was also in the Central School Band and Marching Band. That kept me busy since after school we would do extra-curricular activities like marching, practicing and just having a ball!

I met Tom Rowe during the first few days of school. After the school bus left us off at Central School to begin our day of educational enlightenment, we had to file into the auditorium to wait for the bell to ring to go up to our home rooms. I was sitting in the 6th row of the auditorium and suddenly I noticed a clarinet case sitting next to this young gentleman in the row in front of me… Tom Rowe. I eased up so I was just behind him and said to him, 'Is that a clarinet?' He didn't answer since he was in a heated discussion with the student sitting beside him. Again, I asked the same question… and again… Finally, he turned around and said, 'Yes, this IS a clarinet… satisfied!?' Tom and I became best friends through music, Boy Scouts, going on camping trips with his parents, Bud and Thoma Rowe and just all-around buddies through whatever.

THE ENTICEMENT OF SPORTS

I kept kneading and prodding Dr. Reeves to do more in school as for as for sports is concerned. I just loved to run! He finally gave me permission to play fullback on the Walton Junior High Soccer team. I explained to him there wouldn't be much running involved since basically, all the fullback does is protect the goal.

On our last game of the season, October 1966, the Walton Junior High Soccer Team was playing the Webster Junior High Soccer Team. Time was running out and we were ahead. Someone from Webster kicked this line-drive soccer ball towards the goalie, Brian Lambert. It was coming right towards me, and I had to do something! The soccer ball was going to smash me in the face! I knew the goalie probably wouldn't retrieve the ball if it got that close to the goal. Consequently, I headed the ball in the opposite direction! Both teams stopped in awe and a Webster Junior High Soccer team forward said, 'What a head!!!'

After the 'head' I was so disheveled and wobbly, and I really had a hard time to hide it. I didn't want anyone to see it. I felt like passing out! This could have been the precursor to the happening. Jarring and exasperating a couple of blood vessels in my skull that finally led to my demise.

Participating in a school sports program also brought other benefits... Girls! Young women would be naturally attracted to young men who served on any type of sport team. I don't know why but it was just the culture back then. And girls seem to have a fascination to me much more than before. Maybe it's their uniqueness or unrivaled quality or their importance in life.

It was a hot and muggy summer night in 1966. All us kids, around 13 – 14 years old, were utterly complaining about the weather and it was so hot and sticky. All of a sudden, my mother exclaimed, 'Why don't I take you over to Tripp Lake for a swim!?' It was 8:30 PM and it was just after sunset. All of us were delighted! Pam and I got dressed in our bathing suits and put some clothes on top the bathing attire. Phil Macomber, Diane Macomber, Robin Sawyer and I hopped in the car at our residence and my mother drove to their houses to get changed.

Tripp Lake was about 12 miles from our house located in Mechanic Falls ME. They have a beautiful, sandy beach which everyone flocks to during the summer months. We drove down for about 7 or 8 miles to Mechanic Falls. Then, took a left and hooked for a 5-mile drive to Tripp Lake. All the young women in the car were beginning to blossom into preadult hood. All of them had protruding curves in just the right places.

We got there and went down to the beach. Phil and I had regular bather suits of the time. When Pam and Diane undressed, they had two-piece bathing suits which was a little bit liberal for the time in question. But when Robin Sawyer undressed it was the coming thing… a bikini! I've seen pictures of them, but I never thought I would see one one-on-one. Did that ever get my hormones charging! The bikini had violet and navy-blue flowers on it on a creamy white background. There was nothing to it!

We swam in the water for 10 or 15 minutes. Then, someone saw a float in the water about 40 feet out. We asked Mom if we swim out to it. She said, 'Sure, I'm right here watching you!'

Every time Robin dove off the float I just assumed that something on her bikini would fly off! And when she got up on the float by a ladder… I 'd observe her with droplets of water falling off her bikini and 'the shake' that she produced walking on the float (or anywhere for that matter). It was quite a night and a half. I was getting older, and I knew the draw young woman had on me. It was going to be interesting and electrifying during my high school years!

During the winter of 1966, the Sports Director of Walton Junior High School decided to have a Sports Jamboree at the Walton Junior High Gym. The jamboree was going to be in the evening so parents could and witness, too, beside students. I was one of 4 students picked by the Sports Director to participate in the shuttle run. The director must have known something as far as my physical fitness was concerned. Shuttle run tests usually involve continuous running back and forth between two-line markers at a certain pace, and vary in degrees of intensity, duration, and distance. This shuttle run test was short and quick since he had many drills with other students to perform that night. They are designed to evaluate a competitor's speed and agility.

I practiced for the run. One thing I noticed during my sessions was that the gym floor was awfully slippery. Every time I slowed up to pick up a satchel I either slid or lost my balance. I thought to myself, 'There must be some way to counteract this obstacle.' I tried different methods, and I finally found one that worked well.

Before the race began, I licked my righthand with spit and placed it on the bottom of my sneakers. That gave me a firm grip and footing so I wouldn't slide when I went to pick up the satchel.

I had my parents and Pam at the gym and all my cohorts were there too competing in different events. All of us knew who was going to win…at least most of us thought. There was one competitor who was bragging that he was the fastest person alive, and he was going to win hands down.

There we were, about 20 feet apart, waiting for the gun to go off. 'Bang' and we were off for the race of my life! I ran down and picked up the first satchel…no problem with sliding. All the muscles in my body were pushed to the limit! I had Rick Grant as my tutor or handler pushing me on! And finally, when my last satchel was placed in the race…a thunderous ovation and roar came from the crowd! When I began pacing back to my place in the gym, I went right by Rick Grant. He reached and shook my hand and then slapped me on the back and said, 'Good job!!!' I thought to myself, 'That's odd for Rick (one of my other best buddies in school) to be doing that?' I trotted back to my place on the gym floor and everyone there was shaking my hands and saying, 'Good job!!! How to fire!!' I finally caught my breath and yelled over to Tom Rowe, 'Who won, anyway!?' He said, 'You did… you won the race by 4 lengths!!!' I couldn't believe it!! I knew I loved to run but to win the shuttle run race was too good to be true. It was truly an amazing day!

My sophomore year at EL was not too exciting. School work, the Edward Little High School Band kept me busy. And a new phenomenon was coming on the market… calculators! It was something to do with new digital technology. I thought to myself, 'Interesting… '.

About 2 weeks before my gripping and physical event, the EL Football Coach, Mr. Hersom, wanted a Spring practice of all the boys who were thinking of playing football this coming Fall of 1967. Boy, was I excited! I really wanted to compete and really liked football!

I had basically received the 'green light' from Dr. Reeves on playing non-contact and contact sports in the different school sports programs! When the afternoon came (after high school was over for that day) there were 35 – 40 young men anxiously waiting to try out. The coaches had the try outs in the largest study hall they could muster. The gym had already been assigned to some other sporting event. The High Football coach took the best next thing… study hall. Incidentally, it was also raining outside!? In addition, just before the tryouts, the boys had to shove the folding chairs back aways so us receivers would have a place to run and catch the football.

All the receivers had a chance to catch a couple of balls thrown by the quarterback. I, being young but not too naive, could tell the quarterback was throwing balls right on the mark to last year's teammates and people he wanted on the team. If he didn't know you or he thought you was a loser… he would throw the football way in front, behind or way over your head so you couldn't catch the ball!

I recognized this. All of us had two attempts at catching the ball. My first try the quarterback through behind me. No chance of catching that football! I had to wait in line for about 10 minutes until my last and final try came up.

I thought to myself, 'I don't care how or where he throws… I'm going at it since this is my last shot! The football was upped, and I ran out about 25 feet and took a left hook. I looked at the quarterback and the football was going to go way over my head! I faded out and then jumped to high heavens! I got my fingertips on it but couldn't bring it into my clutches. When I came down from my leap, I landed on 5 or 6 folding chairs! What a racket! Mr. Hersom came running over and said, 'Are you alright??!' I said, 'Yes… but the quarterback through the ball so high I had to go for it!!' The coach said, 'Don't worry… we've got our eyes on you!' That made my chest hair stand on end! It was a dream that never came to pass.

THE EVENT

The home was quite crowded that night. Everyone was over since my Grandparents on my mother's side were there for the weekend. Bumpy, which all his grandchildren called him… Brownie, which his friends called him and Nanny (Lottie) my grandmother. And a few kids about 14-15 years of age were hanging out. The reason being my father had just trekked off to Fort Drum, Thursday, May 18, 1967, for a two (2) week stint since he was in the Army Reserves.

The date was Saturday, May 20, 1967. I had been enjoying everything all day from mowing the lawn, rototilling in the vegetable garden with a front-end tiller, hitting the tennis ball against the barn door since I made the Varsity Tennis Team for Edward Little High School during my Sophomore year.

After supper that evening, 'Bumpy' (Edward P. Weston, Grandfather on my mother's side of family), Phil Macomber and I went out to Taber's to hit a couple buckets of golf balls on the fairway.

Bumpy got me interested in golf 3 or 4 years ago. It was a non-competitive sport, and my parents had to pass it through Dr. Reeves to get an 'OK'. He thought briefly about it and said, 'I don't see any harm in it'.

I didn't like it at first. Every golf ball I hit was either a grounder or a line drive! The golf ball was supposed to be a high arcing ball that eventually made into a hole on the golf green.

This was the first time either of us, Bumpy and I, had taken advantage of a beautiful night and gone out and shot golf balls that year. 'Taber's' was the place to be since everybody brought everybody out there because they had miniature-golf, a 3-hole golf course in another section, an eatery that you could die for, homemade ice cream, a batting practice cage, and finally, all the teenagers who went to High School in the surrounding area of Lewiston-Auburn (Twin Cities) congregated at Taber's… real Exciting!!!

I kind of had to keep a close eye on Bumpy since his right shoulder, bursitis, came at random. But he was still walloping the golf balls out into the green, grassy meadow! Phil did a good job in parking them down fairway, too.

I was a different animal and model, and I loved competitions! I adored the outside! I loved riding my bike, playing backyard football and baseball, skiing and running. Dr. Edward Reeves was in my way since I was a rheumatic fever survivor in the summer of 1963. Then finally, after compelling him time after time, Dr. Reeves gave the 'green light' to participate in non-contact and contact sports at EL. I had been working out to build my physique at Edward Little (EL) and at my own at home for about 6-7 months.

I kept in mind all the different goals in golf such as body posture, where to place your feet and the one important concept was to 'keep-your-eye-on-the-ball'!

Thus, in my little cubicle I placed the golf ball on the golf tee… I teed up next to the golf ball and let it rip! The high arcing golf ball must have gone 290 yards! And I teed up the next, and the next and so and so forth. I thought to myself that with all the physical workouts, stretching, increased muscle mass must be paying off! Bumpy was in the next golf cubicle to me and he couldn't believe how well I was doing!

We brought our empty baskets to the 'Caddy Shack' and headed back to 80 Manley Road, Auburn ME. I told Bumpy and Phil that I had to go on my nightly jog. It shouldn't take long and then I had some homework to complete for Monday morning. Phil wanted to go with me on my run. Phil and I were great friends and co-owners of a large newspaper route.

So, when we arrived home Phil and I talked about it. I didn't want him to run alongside me since he hadn't built up running a long distance. The running course distance was around a mile. But this particular run was different, atypical and devastating.

Thus, I had Phil take my newspaper route bike which was a 2-speed Schwinn, and he could follow me during my run.

I started out from the front porch, took a left on Manley Road, took a right on Rodman Road, then, took a right onto Hotel Road, a right onto Minot Avenue, a right onto Nickerson Avenue, another left onto Manley Road and then basically… home. Phil later said he couldn't keep up with me on the bike since I was running too fast!

I was deliberating during my run of everything that happened last night.

Friday evening, about the time I was getting ready for bed at night, 4 or 5 cars showed up and parked in front of our driveway. The doors opened and about 12 – 16 teenagers all around my age poured out of their cars. It was all over my girlfriend, Nancy, and one of the guys there was Tom Maloney.

Tom Maloney wanted me to cast Nancy aside and let him go steady with her. I said, 'We're having a real good time together, so, why don't wait your turn!' They weren't too pleased with that logical answer. They said, 'Wait until Monday and we'll see what develops from there!' They got in their cars and peeled off! I walked up the driveway to the house. My mother and Pam were waiting and asked me what was on. I said, 'Just a little spat about Nancy. Nothing to worry about.'

Nancy told me later that they came there for a fist fight. But when Tom Maloney saw me walking down the driveway, he had a different thought. I had a body physique that just a few students at EL had. When I came strutting down the driveway with my white t-shirt and Bermudas and then was accompanied with untied sneakers… my heftiness was in full bloom because of the anticipation of the situation.

I was also thinking about Nancy. She was a hot number to come by. We met in Geometry class, and she sat right behind me. Sometimes we 'cheated' during a quiz, in that she would look at my quiz paper for the answer.

Nancy was always joking around and always full of the latest gossip. Nancy was vibrant, fun to be with and bubbling with delight!

'What was going to happen on Monday? Who and where would I confront? What about Nancy? How was I going to keep her as a 'steady'?' I was contemplating all these various factors.

Just as I was about to turn onto Manley Road from Nickerson Avenue, I increased my speed like I always do for the last 100 – 200 yards before my side porch door. All the while thinking about last night, and the ramifications Monday could bring.

Without warning… I had a perturbing and ghostly phenomenon occur in my head. It was an excruciating pain!!! It felt and eminenced like a sword piercing my head!! It lasted for 3-5 seconds, and then… it was gone! I was 15 and couldn't fathom what this episode was all about. I thought maybe it was a migraine headache. I never had one so I couldn't be sure about this mêlée. As far as I knew, everything was kosher since the 'headache' had already disappeared. I said to myself, 'Well, I'm still running and everything else on my body seems to be OK…' but it still troubled me. I ran up to the front porch door… Mom was at the kitchen sink doing dishes… When I entered the screened-in porch, Mom asked, 'How was your run???' And Out of breadth, I said 'Fine!'

I went into the porch and through the kitchen/dining area. I sat down on the den chair. About a minute later my life was transformed.

I must have passed out for 10-15 seconds. The next thing I knew I was leaning heavily on my right side. Phil Macomber was sitting right across from me. He tried to get my attention by saying, 'Jim, Jim… You alright??' And he started waving and making a fuss so as to get a response from me! Then he started shouting, 'Mrs. Hakala, Mrs. Hakala, Mrs. Hakala – Something is wrong with Jim!!!?'

Bumpy was sitting right beside me and felt his hands reach over and steady me so I was still in an upright seated position. That, in itself… was comforting. Mom came into the den and looked at me and tried to converse with me, but I gave no response. I just beheld and looked up intently at her.

My mother told Phil and Bumpy to help me into the living room and lay me on the couch, and turn, she would call up Dr. Reeves.

Phil was on my right side and Bumpy was on my left side. When they aided me from the den to the living room it was only 15 – 20 feet. The first few feet went OK, but Phil lost his grip attempting to hold my right arm on top his shoulder. He sort of lost control and containment of me but he finally made a grasp on me which was more robust than first attempt. It must have been awkward for Phil since my right side seemed to be lagging behind… just dead weight. I had no movement on my right side at all. They dragged my right leg and foot into the living room, and somehow, prostrated me on the couch.

I was laying there on the sofa in such a serene mode. Not a care in the world! Dr. Reeves would fix me all up… I thought. He always did and I had full confidence he would do it this time, too. I too knew that something was wrong but for the life of me, I didn't know what or why. With this injury, no one who happened to be at the house that night was baffled, too!

While we were waiting for Dr. Reeves to show several people came into the living room just to see how I was doing and to make sure was comfortable. I believe Pam and Diane Macomber came into the living room and stood at the foot of the divan. They were whispering to each other and heard them say, 'He just lays there and doesn't speak a word.' Mom came in and leaned over me to tell me, 'Everything is going to be alright. Dr. Reeves is on his way.'

Bumpy was quite shaken up! He came four (4) times, and he was closely watched by Nanny. On the fourth time he came and shook me and said, 'Why don't you say something and speak to me!!!' Nanny saw the whole incident and ran in living room and pulled him back. Nanny told Bumpy, 'Can't you see… Jim can't talk!!?' No one knew what happened to me and neither did I!

I heard sirens coming in the distance. I thought, 'Could they be coming for me?' I guess they were when I saw red lights dancing on the beige living room walls.

Dr. Reeves entered the home and apologized for his tardiness. He said in his records he had our address as 80 Manley Street.

Dr. Reeves and the medical team went to that street address first. Dr. Reeves quickly asked if Robert Hakala lived there. They said 'NO!... but there's an 80 Manley Road!' They took off from the street and went to the road address. It was only 3 miles between addresses, but the tension and apprehension must have been at an all-time high in the ambulance that night.

When Dr. Reeves got out of the ambulance at our residence he asked where I was. Mom led him into the living room to the couch and there I lay. Dr. Reeves said, 'What kind of trouble have you got yourself into this time – you little 'monkey'. I don't know if he calls all adolescent patients 'monkeys' or what? It was kind of annoying at first, but it grew on me.

Dr. Reeves did a quick examination of me. I assume he had seen it before. He lifted my left arm up and told me to hold it in place. Then he did the same thing to my right arm... and when he let go of it, my right arm flopped to the cushion on the couch. He shined a flashlight in both of my eyes. Finally, Dr. Reeves took a percussion reflex hammer and tapped me in different places on my body. Then Dr. Reeves leaned forward and said to me, 'You'll be going for a little ride.'

Dr. Reeves went to the kitchen and gathered everyone around. Dr. Reeves said that he would be taking over to CMG (Central Maine General... now it's called CMMC) in an ambulance. Furthermore, he presumed I had a stroke or cerebral thrombosis (nowadays they call it an ischemic stroke) and he was going to take me to the hospital to accomplish some more tests.

The EMT technicians came into the living room with a wheeled stretcher. They carefully (through Dr. Reeves and my mothers' orders) lifted me up off the couch to the stretcher. It was kind of a tight fit maneuvering me around from the living room... to the den... through the dining area... out through the kitchen... onto the side porch... and finally, out to the waiting ambulance. Take note, the ambulances during that period were like hearses of today. There really wasn't that much room to move around.

They wheeled me out on the paved driveway, and I believe there were several people standing alongside the corridor they interlaced. I thought, 'Man, I'm really the center of attention now!' I was feeling prominent at the moment, but I just didn't know what had happened.

Dr. Reeves sat in the front passenger's seat and my mother and an EMT technician rode in the rear beside me. Dr. Reeves told the ambulance driver 'No sirens! The damage has already been done!' Also, he didn't want any further damage to happen on the way over to the hospital by loud noises and commotions.

We were about halfway to the hospital, by the Androscoggin County Courthouse on Main Street in Auburn, when my mother urged Dr. Reeves to come back and view me. He bent over in the ambulance and came to my side. What my mother was so upset about was my face and lips. My face was pale white, and my lips were a dark blue. All Dr. Reeves did was stare. No facial expression or nodding of his head. He turned around and went back to his seat. I assume my brain was starving for oxygen and it just couldn't receive the life-giving element in my current condition.

DEVINE INTERVENTION

The ambulance arrived at CMG Emergency Facility, and I can still feel the ambulance coming to a halt. The EMT Technicians unloaded me from the ambulance. I can still grasp the stretcher wheels rumbling over the paved, hard surface going into the hospital. Once in the hospital, the EMT's wheeled the stretcher over to the side of a long, empty hallway.

They exchanged words with Dr. Reeves and then, suddenly, I was all alone in the massive hallway. I said to myself, 'Great… I'm going to be laying on this stretcher for hours!'

Then… a remarkable and extraordinary event happened. I was laying on the stretcher, and, in an instant, my Spirit was in a cloud, floating at the upper corner of the hallway! I was peering down at a lifeless and motionless form on a stretcher… and it was me.

My Spirit seemed to be in a state of illusion. Everything around me in the suspension was at peace and repose. I was transcendent. I was reticent and I was in my own thoughts and accepted wisdom. I was moving my eyes slowly around the hallway pondering what was going to appear next in my state of awareness. I continued to observe and study the body for 15-20 seconds.

And then, unexpectedly, a voice came to me. A man's voice… forceful, persuasive and profound. I didn't see a form, figure or shape but the proclamation was commanding.

He said, 'Jim… you can do better than that… !'

After that declaration, I was conveyed back to my body in the twinkling of an eye. I endeavored to look back to see Who said this decree but it happened so quickly. I was absolutely mesmerized by what had just transpired.

One hears of going to other side and the glorious wonders one observes. In the vein of golden streets and arches… walking side by side with Jesus… dancing around in embellished meadows… feasting your eyes on awe inspiring sunrises and sunsets.

The happening was just a dominating pronouncement that I could arise and achieve the unthinkable.

I didn't have too much time to reflect when two (2) medical technicians whisked me off down the hallway into a private hospital room.

REALITY

Waiting there was my mother at the foot of the bed, Dr. Reeves and 3 attending nurses. About 15 minutes later Dr. Rock, a cardiologist, arrived and summated the situation.

The two medical attendants pulled me off the stretcher and put me on to a hospital bed. I let out a mournful cry since they overlooked the fact that I had suffered a right-side ischemic stroke. My right side was completely paralyzed, and they laid my body down on my right arm! I thought I broke it! The pain was immeasurable! My mother yelled out, 'Be careful!!' The nurses rolled me on my left side and took my right arm and hand and placed it gently on my tummy.

Next, I noticed Dr. Reeves doing something on a tray with a conglomeration of needles and syringes. He said, 'Jim, Jim… I'm going to do a spinal tap to see if there's any pressure on your brain. This is going to take a while so lay still!'

Gone… was the word 'Monkey' which usually he parlayed.

Little did I know this was a serious event… a life and death situation. An occasion that nobody wanted to be involved in… including doctors, nurses, EMT's, family and not knowingly…myself!

He laid me over on my right side and inserted the long-needled syringe into the base of my spine. It had been about ten (10) minutes since the needle was stuck into my spine! I just couldn't take it anymore! I started to squirm. Dr. Reeves said, 'I'm almost done Jim. Just be patient!' Patience was not my virtue at the time, and I really began to thrash! He took the needle out and my mother asked what it showed? Dr. Reeves said, 'There is evidence of pressure on the brain.' I thought to myself, 'That's great! What do we do now?'

I laid there in the hospital bed for 2 or 3 minutes and suddenly, I began to projectile vomit all over my lap and on the clean, white, crisp hospital sheets on the bed. I didn't want anyone to witness it. I leaned over to my right side of the hospital bed and continued to projectile vomit all over the floor! Embarrassing or what! I guess you might say I was thinking of my well-mannered self and how I didn't want humankind to behold it.

I realized what I had done and utilized my stomach muscles to swing me back on the bed in an upright seating position. I looked at my mother at the foot of the bed and I lunged towards her in a seating position on the bed. My left arm was in a groping mode while my right arm was retracted and limp behind me. As I leapt, I can recall saying, 'Mom, Mom… what's happening to me?!!!' I later found out that all that came out of my mouth were animal noises and cacophony!

I laid back on the hospital bed with the help of CMG personnel and I slept the night peacefully. Dr. Reeves must have drugged me up to help me calm down, and to take pressure off my brain.

Meanwhile, after I was sedated, Dr. Rock, a cardiologist from CMG, went with my mother down to the basement to make a call to Fort Drum, NY.

Dr. Rock was a Colonel in the same battalion that my father was in. Dr. Rock called Fort Drum Headquarters and asked to speak to Master Sergeant Robert C. Hakala and it was an urgent matter about 10:30 at night. He had the authority to defer my father's outing at Fort Drum.

Dr. Rock and my mother must have waited 10 minutes for my father to come to the phone. My father answered and Dr. Rock told him briefly about the specifics of that night. My mother spoke to my father momentarily and told him to 'get home as soon as possible'. Before my mother hung up the phone, Dr. Rock asked if he could speak to my father once more. Dr.

Rock picked up the receiver and said, 'Bob, drive carefully and don't rush… because your son will be deceased by morning.'

On hearing that, my father went back to the barracks and explained his situation and his predicament to the company troops. Dad asked if there was anyone who could loan him a car to travel back to Maine? A Lieutenant in the barracks said, 'Sure, you can have mine!!'

Dr. Reeves and Dr. Rock told my mother that they would call if anything happened during the night. There was nothing she could do at this point but sit and wait.

I never asked my mother what time she got home that night or if anyone in the house got any sleep. I can't imagine what my mother was reflecting upon when she left the hospital. In fact, I don't even know to this day who brought her home! When she got home and most likely told her parents and probably my sister, Pam, of the events that evening. And was told by Dr. Rock I wouldn't be alive come daylight.

I think it was a surreal experience for everyone that was there that evening. To be waiting for a phone call from the hospital that I had passed away during the night. I do know that different family members looked up 'stroke' and all of its implications in the Encyclopedia Britannica.

Dad didn't give heed of what Dr. Rock said… 'drive carefully'. Dad said he arrived home 5 1/2 hours later from Fort Drum. He told me he was doing 65 mph through Minot Avenue in Auburn ME. The speed limit was 35 mph on Minot Avenue and back then, the Auburn Police Department would give a summons to anyone breaking the speed limit by 2 or 3 mph over what the posted speed would be!

Dad screeched into the driveway at about 7:00 AM the next morning. He pulled up to the house. Got out of his 'loaned' car and Mom met him at the door. Dad stoked his pipe and stood there, and tears came from his eyes. Mom said that was the first and only time she ever saw Dad cry. The first thing my father uttered, 'Is he still alive??' We didn't have any way of communicating back then like we do now…cellphones!

Mom said, 'I haven't heard anything from the hospital!!' Dad said, 'OK… let me have a cup of coffee. We'll go straight over to the hospital after that.'

They filled my father in with all the details of the previous night while he had a cup of coffee. Once he finished his coffee and freshened up, my mother and him rushed over to CMG.

FIRST VISIT

My parents arrived at the hospital about 8:30 AM Sunday morning, May 21, 1967. The first thing they inquired was if I was still alive???

It must have been very difficult for Mom and Dad those few hours before they saw me that morning. Dad hurrying to get home from Fort Drum NY. And Mom who witnessed the whole alarming and perturbing chain of events.

I later found out I awoke about an hour and half earlier before they arrived. I was still under sedation to keep me placid. I was crying and I kept repeating, 'Mom! Mom!… I want my mother!! I want to go home!!' At least I thought that was what I was saying. The nurses told my parents that just wails and moans came out of me!

Finally, a nurse came over to see me and she said, 'You've got visitors!' I was still crying and there were tears coming out my eyes and then saw them… my mother and father coming over to my bedside.

And I said to myself, 'That's Dad! He's not supposed to be here! He's supposed to be at Fort Drum??!' I quickly stopped crying and wiped my eyes of tears and tried to look composed. Back then, males were understood to be the dominant side of humanity!

Mom came up and hugged me! It was kind of odd because I hugged her back with just one arm… my left!? But that didn't matter. At least they were here by my bedside!

Dad asked me, 'How I was doing?' And I said, 'Good!' And he said, 'What did you say?' My speech was beginning to come back, and his question of, 'What did you say?' affected me. And I said, 'Good!' in a more affirmative purpose and tone. He said, 'That's better.' And I nodded my head.

After they visited for about 5 minutes, they said that they had to go and talk to Dr. Reeves about my condition. And I pleaded to them, 'Are you coming back!?' And Dad said again, 'What did you say?' And I said with better pronunciation and distinction, 'Are you coming back?' And Mom said, 'Of course we are. We'll be back this afternoon.'

May 21, 1967, was taken up by doctors, nurses coming to read my vitals, 2 visits by my parents and Dr. Reeves still had me under sedation to keep me solace.

I assume the meetings my parents had with the doctors were one of astonishment and revelation. Given all the symptoms I had that night before, it led the medical profession to believe it was doom and gloom!

During the day, I was in a state of wonderment. Watching the nurses and doctors go hither and thither over the ET floor… peering outside at green, lush front lawn…dozing throughout the day… trying to fathom what in the world happened last night… waiting for Mom and Dad to finally visit for the last time during the sunlight hours.

May 22, 1967, Monday, really didn't bring much of any substance. Same old thing… doctors and nurses coming to my bedside and gawking at me! A couple of visits from my parents but Dr. Reeves still had me sedated.

When no one was around, I lay on the crisp, clean and white sheets, made sure I was laying just right and lifted my left hand no problem. With my unaffected left arm, I raised my right arm at a 45-degree angle from the bed. Then, I let go of my right arm with my left workable side and it just 'plopped' on top of the bed. 'NO can do!' I tried this maneuver 5 or 6 times that day! And it all came out with the same result… 'plop'. I didn't understand the quandary I was in.

I was still sedated and about 3:45 PM EST a nurse came to my bedside and said, 'You've got some visitors!' The nurse brought a bag full of presents.

I looked at the gifts with a wobbly head and I thought to myself, 'What in the world??' I looked the ET Ward over and I didn't see anyone. The nurse said, 'No… they're right over there.' The floor was arranged in a black and white checkerboard pattern. She used her index finger to point, and I thought she was pointing at a tile square in the middle of the ET Ward floor!

She said, 'Let me help you!' She positioned herself so she could get me in a seating position. I was still looking at the tile square and I was sort of in a daze. The nurse said, 'Up by the entrance door to the ET Ward!' I bobbled my head and finally saw them.

It was my 3 best friends from Edward Little High School… Tom Rowe, Joanne Demers and my girlfriend, Nancy Chesley. They were waving and smiling and wishing me well. All I could muster was a half-hearted wave and I smiled. I think the smile did me in. My left-side of my mouth was a normal smile but the right-side of my mouth was lethargic and motionless. I opened the gifts while they were watching, and I was so gratified.

I forgot who told me this, but he/she said when they moved back into hallway, they all got into a circle with arms around each other and cried. They kept saying to each other, 'Is he going to be alright?? Will he ever be alright???' They had just witnessed a stunning shock and realized that when they saw me, I wasn't the former Jim. It was a new and distinct Jim that I would have to get a hold of.

At the time, I was 15, I didn't view it in this way. I just thought 'woe-is-me' and that's just the way I regarded it. It wasn't until later in years I advocated my limitation as a gift from God and I thanked Him for the challenge.

The presents from my dear friends—I still have them to this day. On the fourth day, May 24, 1967, the doctors took me off the sedatives. I wasn't as drugged as I had been previously. I was making some progress with my spontaneous recovery from the stroke. I was speaking much better, and a little movement was coming to my right-hand limbs.

Pam, my sister, who was 14 months younger than I, wanted to come up to see me with my parents. My parents were elated that she wanted to! I was still mentally, in disarray. My processing and cognitive analysis were still disoriented.

Mom, Dad and Pam came up about 4:00 PM. Pam was so excited and thrilled to see me. Also, I imagine, she was a little apprehensive.

During their visit a Cafeteria Assistant came over with my evening meal. I had to eat with my left hand. My dominant side was the right side of my body before the ischemic stroke. Thus, I was quite clumsy and unpolished in eating with my left hand. But who cares! I could actually devour real food! It wasn't much but it tasted so good!

After the meal was just about over, I had some sliced peaches on my tray. I also had salt and black pepper packets. I looked at the one packet labeled 'black pepper' and asked Mom to open it for me. Once she opened the packet, she handed it back to me… I peppered the sliced peaches!? Pam saw this and thought I had lost it! She turned around from my bedside and walked out of the ET ward.

I realized what I had done but it was too late to bring it back. I knew I had upset all three of them, but I couldn't differentiate any better at the time. I really couldn't say anything since my speech just wasn't there.

The sliced peaches were great but a little on the bitter side!!

COMPREHENSION... I CAN'T READ

The next day Mom came alone. Somehow, I asked her where Dad was. She said he was back at work.

Thinking back can you conceive what thoughts and feelings were going through my parents' minds? I cannot! Their mindset and emotional state must have been resolute and solid! To have a son who was on his way to becoming a strong and colorful young adult, and then, to be walloped with all things... a stroke!?

The Lord has his plans, his itinerary, his arrangements for every human being on this earth. It's just up to 'us' to make the right choice in this perplexing world of our individual selves.

However, on my mother's last visit for the day she asked me if there was anything I wanted from home. I thought for a moment, and I said, 'Comic books!?'

The next day arrived and here comes Mom loaded down with a grocery bag full of comic books! I was so elated! Mom stayed for about 20 minutes, and I couldn't wait to read 'Superman'!

I picked up the comic book. On the front cover it had a picture of Superman flying off a building to the rescue! I said to myself, 'This ought to be good!' I had only read the comic about 10 times before! I opened the first page and started to read. At least I thought I could read?!

It didn't make sense! I looked at the second page and the written words were again, all scrambled! Then I fast forwarded to Page 14 and still, the same thing! I thought the publishers had made a misprint! But I've read this Superman comic book several times before!

I picked up a different comic and the same thing occurred. It was like you see a sentence that orates 'I saw Sally run!' To me… it would come out in my perception, 'I run Sally saw!' and even that was difficult to get my thinking and thoughts around!

It was discouraging, frustrating and confusing! I could partially read individual words but to put them into sentence… it was unworkable! I couldn't read! It was demoralizing! I put the comic book down on top of the pile of comics and just stared out of the window onto the green, front lawn of Spring.

I was stunned! Just stared out of the window and thought to myself, 'What has this 'stroke' done to me?' It wasn't until a couple of days later when my mother asked me, 'How are your comic books?' Meaning, was I enjoying reading my comic books? I just shook my head, and I said simply, 'I can't read…'

What had happened to me was a condition called Alexia. Alexia is an acquired deficit in the ability to understand written language. Alexia emanates in three main forms 1) central 2) posterior 3) anterior alexia's. The language cortex nerve in the brain attains impairment. Personally, I was affected by all three levels in various ways. Alexia comes in different scenarios where the letters are all mixed up, you can't pronounce vowels, you can't read out loud, the inability to comprehend spelled words and etc.

About the same time as these additional afflictions were occurring… a new one came to surface… aphasia. During that time in the 1960's they just termed it, simply, as aphasia. Nowadays, speech or language pathologists have 7-12 different aphasia's that are everyday terminologies. I will touch on two which I know I had which are the most basic: 1) Broca aphasia and 2) transcortical motor aphasia.

Broca's aphasia suggests a stroke survivor knows what he wants to say and one afflicted with this can comprehend what others are saying. Nevertheless, language is laborious, and it requires great application.

I can remember when I was in Mr. Jenkin's Algebra II class during the Junior year of EL. I was sitting my seat and Mr. Jenkin's asked this same question 3 different ways on an 'abstract value equation'. Out of 30 students in class, no one raised their hands with an answer. I knew the correct answer when Mr. Jenkins first asked it. I was contemplating and thinking how I was going to say that 'word' or 'words' to answer the question.

I didn't want to mess up the sentence and have all the students in his class treated with disdain and roll in the aisles. Finally, I raised my hand and Mr. Jenkins said, 'Yes!!??' I gave the answer which was correct. And he said, 'At least with one student in this class is paying attention!'

When I got home that afternoon, I told my mother about it. She was thrilled that I actually made an effort in high school to further my recognition both socially and intellectually.

Getting back to the subject, transcortical motor aphasia is a different mode of aphasia. One can understand language but can't communicate fluently. One can use short phrases, have a delayed response time and frequently repeat things.

I can reminisce the time my girlfriend, Nancy Chelsey, came to visit me with my parents a couple of weeks after the event. I was still in CMG and was nervous but elated she was coming. My parents and her came into my room and I hugged her with one arm! All of us exchanged cordialities and my parents left Nancy and me alone to be with each other.

Nancy was quite a natural chatterbox, and we talked about our friends, school, social life, when I was getting out of the hospital etcetera. Again, she talked a lot and there was no pressure for me to say that much. But once in awhile I would try to express or input something to the conversion and I would say, 'I think, I think, I think, I think!?' I said to myself, 'Where did that come from??' It was embarrassing, humiliating and disconcerting. No one in the professional medical community told me I had transcortical motor aphasia. I presumed it was too novel at the time to put an appellation on it.

I was very self-conscious and insecure at this time. I accepted what happened to my physical self. I saw others in school, in town and/or in the grocery store and they were doing the same motor mechanisms that I used to do but I couldn't do it now. I didn't have the same thought process that I do at this writing. The stroke was a gift from the Lord above that I should have realized at the time.

Everyone poised around me doesn't even know or comprehend what I had to go through to become what I am today. Nowadays, one sees TV commercials concerning desperate individuals who are without an arm or a leg or going through a number of operations and beseeching for assistance to their organizations.

These individuals truly do have a mountain to climb. A person, similar to my affliction, has a bigger summit to resolve. As far as answering my right arm and leg to respond correctly, I had the task of learning how to communicate, orate and decipher letters and numbers and musical notes that crafted me to be a somewhat of a normal person.

It makes me wince every time I see an infomercial like this because it brings back memories of what I had to go through.

I would enjoy giving them every red cent I had to these proud organizations… but on the other hand, I've got my family, my peers and myself to reflect upon and care for. I presume one just says, 'Continue…in this magnificent world called 'life' and you'll see what's around the next bend!'

WHAT WENT WRONG

I heard doctors, nurses and even my parents talking about 1) cerebral angiopathy and 2) physical therapy. The doctors were really anxious for the cerebral angiopathy since they wanted to find out what happened in my brain. Cerebral angiopathy is a dye they put in your blood vessels by way of a catheter. It aids them in pinpointing the blockage in my brain by color contrast. After this was completed Dr. Reeves would schedule me for Physical Therapy.

It was about a week when I had the cerebral angiopathy test accomplished. The medical assistants wheeled me into a room on a stretcher. They helped me relocate to a flat table. The X-Ray Technician was a beautiful woman. All the curves in the right places! I mean she was absolutely gorgeous! The first thing she had me do was strip! I motioned to her, 'You mean everything!?' And she said in a professional way, 'Yes.'

I mean I was almost at the peak of my hormonal manifestation! I was so worried that I was going to get an erection of the penis that I turned beet red all over my body!

Three days later, I awoke from my coma. The doctors told my parents during the cerebral angiopathy test, a coma sometimes happens in cases like this.

I had lost all the spontaneous recovery from my ischemic stroke. I had to start out all over again! It was like commencing from square one. I surmise it's more difficult attempting to regain the function of motor movements than have the spontaneous recovery facilitating you along the way. On a scale from 1 to 10, I believe my spontaneous recovery was a 3. After the Cerebral angiopathy, it was at a devastating 1!

I still had my memory… I could still focus… I still had my intellect. I had a deviated tongue which is common amongst stroke survivors. To put it in more simply terms the right-hand section of my tongue was semi-paralyzed. But to employ and utilize my motor movement muscles that I had gained back during spontaneous recovery just vanished.

The tongue is responsible for all the words which come out of your mouth and it's also muscle. It wasn't until 5 or 6 months later when I discerned the value of a book called 'Roget's Thesaurus (RT)'. I haven't told anyone until this writing, but Roget's Thesaurus was invaluable and instrumental in communicating with the human race.

Whenever I knew what I wanted to say but the word was difficult to conform my tongue around… the Roget's Thesaurus was there to articulate synonyms that my tongue could assimilate.

For example… I want to voice the word 'run'. Run was challenging to conform my tongue around. I'd look it up in the RT, 'run', and it would give me synonyms for 'run' such as dart, prance, dash, jog and etc. I would practice with my tongue and mouth until I found a word that I could pronounce with no stuttering, faltering or hesitating. I could communicate using that synonym 'jog' with no difficulty and convey my message.

Some people thought I was absurd, ludicrous, unintelligent and/or mindless. But I knew what the Roget's Thesaurus was all about. It helped me to navigate through society. It facilitated me to converse with my family, friends, acquaintances, and life.

For that reason, language is the heart and soul of the mental process and dominance in anyone's existence. My cerebral angiopathy was realized. I really was disheartened with the results on my physical body. I could do hardly a thing as far as motor movements on my right side were concerned. All the doctors, nurses and family were trying to give me encouragement since physical therapy was right around the corner.

Little did they know how I felt, since they were not experiencing or subjected to an ischemic stroke of my caliper. But I was optimistic since that was what life was all about... expectations, promise and hope.

The morning came for my first session of physical therapy. My mother introduced me to a wheelchair. She got me established on the manual wheelchair... my right arm in my lap... my right foot on the foot stand. And we're off!

It was actually fun being transported to the physical therapy session in a wheelchair! Mom was whooshing me down through the hallways! The air blowing through my hair and in hopeful anticipation this type of therapy was going to be an answer to this crippling event.

When we arrived at the Physical Therapy (PT) Ward, PT Head Nurse, Mrs. Longhorn, PT Assistant, Mrs. Barre and another PT Assistant, Theresa, were there to greet me. Mrs. Longhorn went all through the protocols and regulations before we began. Mrs. Longhorn assigned Theresa to give me my first Physical Therapy workout.

Theresa said that they would begin on my right leg. Mom and Theresa gently pulled me out of my wheelchair and placed me on a flat, padded worktable. Theresa said she was going to straighten out my leg... lift it up to a 45- or 50-degree angle... . And push down! Once she had my right leg in the air to push down, I was to use all the strength I could muster and push up to make leg straight again.

She got up on table with me... did everything she said she was going do to. One minor altercation. When she pushed down on my right leg... she slammed it down!! The pain was immense! And she said, 'PUSH!!' I pushed as hard I could but only a feeble nerve impulse was there. Then she said, 'Let's do it another time.' I thought she was saying, 'That's good. Let's do it another day'. But 'NO!'. She hopped up onto the table again and we did it a second time. We did the exercise 10 times! But each time I had a better nerve impulse than the last. I knew the pain that came from doing this exercise, so I prepared and mitigated for it. The tribulation got less and less through time so that was conciliating.

I spent an hour down in therapy. Theresa put my legs, arms, foot and hand/fingers in every imaginable position. I was gratified when the session was over. My mother wheeled me out of the physical therapy ward and back to my room.

When she stopped the wheelchair in my room… I cried! I must have had tears welling up in my eyes for 10 minutes. Mom was trying to console me. I couldn't say to her what I was feeling because of my speech impediment… to tell her, 'This is going to be a long process. My future was looking dubious. You don't know how much that hurt me during that PT session. But I'm going to exert myself to make a full recovery! And… I love you!'

I went to Physical Therapy 9 or 10 days after the first session. All the identical physical movements day after day after day. What the PT's said and which is true, 'Repetition, Repetition and Repetition! period.'

During this time, I had numerous visitors. I couldn't really say that much but who cares! I care!! When you have a caller, you expect your visit to take place in a normal atmosphere and conversation to be the prevailing theme. It made me very uneasy, edgy and disconcerted since I didn't have any dialect.

I had one teacher from school come over to the hospital during my stay. It was my biology teacher, Mr. LeBlanc. He said the normal things a person would say, and he visited for a few minutes. Nervous…Oh, was I uneasy. I could hardly say a thing and wanted to appear upright and a thankful student. He said the class missed me and he hoped I would soon be up on my feet again.

My private room was on the first floor so I could see all the comings and goings of visitors since the walkway to the hospital's front door was within my sight. I saw him walking down the walkway to his car. He had his head bowed, looking at the walkway and walking with his hands on his waist with suit jacket ruffling behind him. He seemed to be in a thoughtful state and probably contemplating my condition.

The next day of school, I don't know if he told the students in my classroom about the visit or the mountain I had to climb. But it was amiable to see that someone else cared about my plight.

GOING HOME

Doctors and nurses kept coming in and out of my room all day long. Dr. Reeves came in during the late afternoon, 06/08/1967, Thursday. He said, 'You're doing good, you little monkey! I tell you what? If you can go the entire distance of the hallway, up and down, with this full leg brace on… you can go home that day.' I nodded my head in anticipation.

The leg brace was a straight-leg brace which attached to my hip and went straight down to my ankle. A little confining to what I used to doing with my right leg. But I was so excited! I practiced on it for a couple days at physical therapy and I knew I could handle it.

The morning came on June 12, 1967, Monday. Dr. Reeves, my mother, and Mrs. Longhorn, Head of PT, were there. Mrs. Longhorn strapped the brace to my leg in my room. From there I went out to the hallway. I wanted to show all of them what I could do. So, I looked up into the hallway to see the distance I had to travel.

And there at the end of the hallway were two (2) of my nurses that took care of me while I was in hospital. They were sweet and so delightful! And they were quite attractive, too! I had regained a small part of my motor movements on my right side. I had a cane that supported me on my left side for balance, plus, a straight-leg brace on my right side.

I was nervous. All these officials (even my mother) were watching me, and I knew I had to deliver and achieve something of the highest caliper. I took the first step, and everything went haywire!

I had no control over the muscles I had regained use of! My right arm and hand went flying up into the air! I wanted to bring it down with my left hand, but I couldn't do that because I was holding a cane with my left side. During the first few steps… I stopped. I thought to myself, 'What's more important at this moment… going home or staying in the hospital?' I did alright in my PT sessions practicing with this leg brace since I knew them, and they knew what I was going through. Why now? It suddenly hit me! I was self-conscious… keenly aware that other people were evaluating and observing me, and I didn't like or want that! I knew what I could do but I had no idea I couldn't control and restrain my muscles as I did in the past.

Mom said, 'What's the matter Jim? Go on! You can do it!'

I took each perturbing and tormenting steps down the hallway… turned around… and limped back to the starting point. When I almost there I looked up and Dr. Reeves was smiling and my mother said, 'Good job!!' Dr. Reeves said, 'I'll do the paperwork! You little monkey… you're going home!'

I can recall the exit from CMG. A nurse took me down in a wheelchair to the car with my mother right along my side. When we arrived at the car, I wasn't sure what to do. I never practiced with the PT's getting out of a wheelchair and into an automobile. I was aided by the nurse and my mother to stand up. I made my way to the car which was just a few steps, and my right leg began to buckle. I was scrupulous and didn't want anyone to assist me! Me, myself and I caught myself from falling down! I made it to the passenger's side front door and swung around to seat myself in the passenger's seat. The nurse lifted my right leg into the car, and she said, 'Are you all set?' I looked up at her and nodded my head. And she gave the parting words, 'Good luck!!'

The way home was surreal! It was only 2.9 miles between CMG and home! I really couldn't believe it! All the cars, traffic, congestion and people walking to do whatever in their busy sphere of life. Everything was so green and lush since we were just a week away from summer! When my mother drove up into the driveway we entered the half-circled drive next to the garage. My father always said he wanted a circle 'something' in his driveway. We parked right in front of purple lilac, Syringa vulgaris, that was just in bloom. It was so beautiful, rich, green, creamy, purple flowers were blooming everywhere. It was good to be back home!

I opened up the passenger's front door and my mother said, 'Wait a minute, Jim!' She came rushing over to my side of the car to help me out. With a cane in my left hand and Mom supporting me on my right side, I hobbled up to the house which was only 35 feet away. Dad was working and Pam, my sister, was in school and finishing up the last year at Walton Junior High School.

Eventually, I settled down in the living room and sat comfortably in a chair and watched television. I tried to eavesdrop on my mother since she made quite a few calls to family and friends. But I just caught pieces and tidbits of the conversation. Essentially, everyone was glad I was home, and they couldn't believe that I survived such an immense ordeal!

Dad came home about 1:15 PM on a stopover on his regular route. He was a U.S. Mail Contractor, and he always did this 6 days a week. When he entered the home, he met Mom at the door and he said, 'Is he home??' Mom said, 'Yes!!!' He washed his hands in the kitchen sink as always. He usually had a sandwich and cup of coffee before he made last trip with the mail up to West Bethel ME.

He came into the living room and said, 'How does it feel to be home?' Mind you, I could hardly talk at all. I could say individual words with just a little bit of impedance but that was just about it. So, I said, 'Good!' He continued chatting with me for a few minutes. But then he had his lunch and off to work he went for the afternoon.

Pam got off the school bus around 2:45 PM. I had anticipation of seeing my sister again since it had been about 3 weeks since I had not been confined to a hospital bed. I can remember seeing her walk up the driveway through the living room window. The look of reflection and hopefulness was on her face. She entered the house and Mom was talking on the phone. Pam set her paraphernalia from school on the dining room table. Mom said over the phone, 'I gotta' go! My daughter just arrived from school!' Pam said to Mom, 'Is he home?' Mom said, 'Yes, he's in the living room!' Pam and Mom came in and talked for about 10 or 15 minutes. Pam talked about school and all the jibber-jabber.

Mom was serious about the directions she received from PT. I was an outpatient, now. PT dictated to Mom (and me) I was to lay the floor and do these repetitive exercises 3 times a day. In due course, they went into the dining area and talked some more. I tried to be an earwig, but I was so drained of the events of day I kept dosing off the rest of the afternoon. Pam and Mom were busy on the phone that afternoon. They kept coming to check on me from time to time. Asking me if I needed anything and if I was feeling OK.

Nighttime finally set in. My father arrived back to the house about 6:45 – 7:00 PM from his West Bethel ME trip. The family would settle down to a nice evening meal. Everyone was so concerned about my traditional place at the table. I sat on the furthermost point of the dining room table. It was a little squeeze getting over there even for a normal person. They took out all the dining room chairs, and I shuffled my way over to my place at the kitchen table. Then, it came to eating the meal.

No one had ever seen me eating with my left hand. Eating was always done with my dominant side... my right hand. I was still imprecise and clumsy when it came to eating anything with my other side. And I was aware the family was watching me!

We had ham steak, macaroni and cheese and all things... green peas! Mom cut up my ham steak. Dad was sitting at the opposite end of the dining room table. He kept glancing at me as the meal progressed.

Pam was an eagle eye! She observed every move I made! She was bringing a portion of ham to her mouth. When she was half-way to her mouth... she stopped. She was looking at me while placing some macaroni and cheese in my mouth. I could see her making different motions with her mouth hoping I would get it in my mouth with no alterations! When I did make the victuals safely to my mouth, I gathered a big 'sigh' overtook my whole family!

I was so vulnerable and unconfident in myself, that's the way it appeared to me. And then the green peas!? I tried eating them with a fork. The green peas would just roll off my fork. Then Dad mentioned, 'Try a spoon.' I attempted eating the green peas with my spoon and the peas would fall off my plate and onto the floor! Mom said, 'That's OK, I'll get them after the meal'. Thus, eating at the dining room table was quite an assignment for me during the next several weeks.

At the time, I couldn't tell anyone about their misdemeanors at the dining room table since I couldn't talk in a fluent manner. To me, every time I tried to talk, I stumbled all over the discourse. But as long as one practices and does it in repetition, anything you try to accomplish… you will get better at it!

It had been a long day. The family eventually went into the living room to watch television for the evening. We watched TV for about an hour and then it was time to get ready for bed.

One problem… my bedroom was on the second floor. Our full bathroom was also on the second floor.

How was I going to get upstairs? I couldn't take stairs as of yet. Not knowing, my mother and father had already discussed this matter. When I arrived at the bottom of the stairs… I looked up and saw the formidable task facing me. Dad said, 'You ready?' I looked at him in a questionable way. My father said, 'I'm going to carry you up the stairs!' He draped me in his arms, and he carried me up the flight of steps! And I thought to myself as he brought me up the staircase… 'One problem solved.' On the other hand, I knew I had a lot more obstacles to unscramble in this fascinating continuation called life.

After about a week I had had enough of this! I told my parents I wanted to go up the stairs 'one at a time'. They said, 'OK, we'll try it. But your father has to be right in back of you in case you lose your balance.' I made it up the stairs and my parents were quite impressed. In 3 or 4 weeks I was taking the staircase like a normal human being. Only one flaw… I dragged my right foot on the instep, riser of the staircase. I guess you'd say, my competitive spirit and self-worthiness as a human being was coming back to play.

MOWING THE LAWN WITH A MTD

About the second or third day of being home Dad asked me what I really wanted to do now that I was home. I motion to him along with saying in broken language, "Mow the lawn."

This was back in 1967. Riding mowers or lawn tractors were becoming a hit in the homeowner's market. They were expensive back then even if you bought a used one. My father knew that I couldn't push a mower since my right arm had to be a sling whenever I went out and I had a difficult time walking. Thus, he went out and bought a used riding mower! If I remember correctly, it was a used MTD!

Dad came in the house one summer afternoon in June and said to me, "I've got a surprise for you and guess what?" Naturally, I said, "What?" He said, "It's outside." We went outside and just off the driveway resting on the lawn was a riding mower! I went over and marveled at it. I went over and gazed at the mower from stem to stern! My father went over the instructions in how to operate the mower and then he said, "Why don't you get on it and try it." And I said, "Me?" He said, "Sure. Just try it."

I finally muddled on to the driver's seat. My Dad picked up my right leg and put it on the mowers deck. The controls on whether you wanted the mower to go forward, neutral or reverse were on the left side of the mower. I thought to myself, *"Great!"* The control on whether you wanted the mower to travel slow or fast was located by a pedal for the right foot on the mower deck. This could be a problem, I said to myself. Dad got a piece of strapping and wound my right foot loosely to the pedal… problem solved. I could apply enough pressure to my right foot to move the pedal back and forth. Dad said, "Start her up!"

I started the mower and revved it up. Once I put it into drive and went ahead two feet my right leg flopped over to the right, and my right leg was literally hanging there. It didn't look good… My father observed and pondered the situation. I looked at him and he said, "Wait one minute and I'll be right back." Dad went to the garage and came back with a section of rope. He tied the rope just above both knees, so it brought my right leg into a resolute driving position. "He said, "Now try it." I went forward a few feet, engaged the rotary mower and mowed and mowed and mowed! Of course, my father was right behind me seeing that nothing got out of kilter, but I didn't care! I was having the time of my life!

Looking back, the scene must have appeared kind of funny and odd for passer-byers to witness a young boy, on a riding mower, a sling on his right shoulder, with a rope encompassing his legs, with a man following him… mowing the lawn! It is laughable to reminisce. I was proud of myself seeing such a minor modification with rope, which has been around for thousands of years, could do so much to an individual's ego.

How little does humanity realize what's going on in each other's minds? It is truly captivating!

SPEECH THERAPY

My mother and I were busy as bees going to PT three times a week. Coming home and doing PT exercises three times a day. During the month of June 1967, my mother enrolled me in Speech Therapy in Lewiston ME. The PT Department at CMG recommended this agency to her since my aphasia was so bad. We went there twice a week in the beginning. I wish I could remember the Speech Pathologists name, but we'll call her Ms. Jones.

Ms. Jones took me through the mill as far as speech was concerned. Ms. Jones had me naming photos and visual scenes. One thing I loathed was she told me a 'phrase' and I had to tell what meant. Like… 'Top of the morning to you!' We all know that's a morning greeting between friends, family members and associates. But to tell her what it meant… that was so difficult. All the words were disorganizing in my mind, and I just couldn't pick them out to circumscribe, describe and express it. I felt stupid and impudent. But on the contrary, I wasn't.

Ms. Jones put me through the formation of sentences. She had me cue in sentences. The cow jumped over the _____. And I would say, "moon." When I finished the sessions, my head would really be spinning!

Just about when the third meeting was just about over. Ms. Jones picked a book up from her desk. She said, "I want you to take this book and open it up from time to time." I told her, "But I can't read!" And even that articulation came out disarrayed. Ms. Jones said, "I know you can't read but take it home and you may be surprised!"

The book was 'The Hobbit' by T.R.R. Tolkien. My mother and I got in the car, and we were just about ready to go home, and Mom said, "What's that in your hands?" I said, "A book." Mom said, "But you can't read!?" I looked at her and then stared out the car window all the way home. When we arrived home, I went upstairs, book in hand, sat in a chair, opened up the book… the first page looked like blur or a distortion to me. I said to myself, 'How in the devil am I supposed to read when the first page looks this… 'mumbo-jumbo'.

We continued to visit Ms. Jones for about two months. Then one day she said the agency lost their funding from the federal government. They were closing the facility at the end of August 1967. The news was very disappointing for me. I believe I had made some progress in my vernacular going to the sessions for speech therapy. But one thing I have to mention…

It was about the middle of August 1967. I was concerned about my Junior year at Edward Little High School. I retained my memory, focus and intellect but I still couldn't decipher anything! I couldn't read a newspaper, a magazine, books, sheet music, letters etc.

I really didn't notice anything on the way over in the car going over to speech therapy. Again, I was put up with that same grueling repertoire of pathology. After it was over, my mother and I took the same route back to home every time we went to their location on Park Street, Lewiston ME.

After the session was finished, we got in the car and pulled onto Park Street. Kennedy Park was just to our left. We stopped at the stop sign at the intersection of Park Street and Chestnut Street and took a right onto Lisbon Street. And I said to myself, 'Something is different?' I couldn't put a handle on it, but something was distinct and unique.

All the neon signs advertising the names of retail stores made sense.

The letters and characters had a purpose and reason behind them. We were just about up to Peck's Department Store on Main Street, and we just passed Grant's Clothing. Grant's Clothing was a men's clothing store that all the high-up young men and menfolk went to for the latest in fashions! I looked at the insignia and actually pronounced the words to myself, 'Grant's Clothing…!' As we passed it, I did a second look just to make sure it was truthful in my mind. It was! The letters formed something I could put a handle on and transformed gibberish into an undeviating, absolute and distinctive word!

I began to get excited! I really couldn't believe it! With more intent, I started becoming aware of the signs on the road like 'STOP' or YIELD'! They meant and implied something to me!

I didn't say anything to my mother but questioned myself if this could be a turning point in my recovery process.

We arrived at the old homestead, and I immediately shot out of the car (in my own way)! I went into the house and hobbled upstairs! I didn't even stop for a 'Get Out of Jail Free' card, either! I entered my bedroom and picked up 'The Hobbit' by T.R.R. Tolkien. I read the first 2 chapters!

I didn't know what it was about. Some of the names and characters were hard to pronounce. And the book really gets involved into a fairyland. Really captivating!

I hurriedly went down the stairs and yelled, "Mom… Mom!!" She said, "What's the matter?" I stood in the laundry room as she folding clothes and said to her, "I can read!!!" She said, "What do you mean You can read!?" I said to her in broken dialect, "I just read the first 2 chapters of 'The Hobbit!"

You do not… I repeat… You do not know and recognize how important and momentous a feeling it is to a person that has been affected with an ischemic stroke like mine with your reading ability just vanishes!

All the therapists, whether it be physical, occupational, neurological or whatever, can't fathom the loss of hope or resiliency it takes away from an individual when you lose something you once had! All your dreams and aspirations dashed in a second! And a stroke victim or a brain-besieged person who has aphasia or alexia is just reaching out and saying, 'Please… Please help me with this affliction!!?' No wonder people suffering post-stroke and other brain maladies have depression and dejection.

They have within themselves a form of grief, melancholy and despair. They say to themselves, 'How can I ever overcome all these impediments?'

DOCTORS WHO MAKE OUTCOMES

Throughout the summer of 1967 my parents had me going to different psychologists, psychiatrists, prosthetists, orthotists, and physiatrists. My mother to several psychologists in their understanding how far would progress as far as mental ability, cognitive areas, focus, memory and concentration. One psychiatrist located in Leeds ME was especially reflective. I wish I could remember his name, but he came down to the conclusion that 1) I would be an average student at Edward Little High School and 2) that would good community college candidate. That didn't set too well with me. And my mother was complaining and criticizing his verdict all the way home.

What really got my dander up was when we went to a Doctor of Physiatrist. A doctor of the trade is renowned for treatment and analysis for coming to a determination of one's physical ability and handling what life shot at you. It took place in the later weeks of July 1967. I remember it was a large room, about 40' X 40'. Just the doctor, my mother and I were there. I assume the Physical Therapy Division at the hospital called him in to do an assessment of my condition. Since, they didn't think I was performing like should be at this crucial point. There was 'one' chair for me to sit down on while he performed his tests in the very center of the room.

He had two (2) instruments in his hands. One being a long needle. The other being a percussion hammer, the type that doctors do a 'reflex' evaluation. Now he said this may hurt in some areas around your body, but it has to be implemented. He poked me in all the different areas around my physique of a frame. Then used the hammer to test my reflexes. I warned him in my own way about my right side and told him it was very sensitive. He finally arrived at my right knee, and he was standing directly in front of me. He gave a mega poke… my right knee zipped out quicker than a rocket! My right foot caught him right in the shin! The doctor showed some discomfort and pain. My mother apologized for me since I couldn't converse that well and I in turn blushed. The physiatrist took me through all the motions of bending my knee, elbow, lifting my right arm, sit-ups and turning from side-to-side both sitting and standing.

He studied his observations and also the Physical Therapy comments at CMG he had in front of him. He looked up at me and said, 'I'm sorry to say you have reached a 'plateau'. I'm discontinuing all further Physical Therapy appointments until you reach a stage where you show improvement.' I said to myself, 'What??? What in tarnation is a 'plateau'??' I mean I was only 16! How in hell am I supposed to discern what 'plateau' implies in this increasing world of medical terminology? And especially in the condition I was in… alexia, broca and transcortical motor aphasia and the like. I knew that plateau insinuated 'flat'. But how was I going to realize what it represented to my human existence? I was a mess!

But my mother knew.

She asked the physiatrist if I could still go to speech therapy sessions? He said, 'Yes. Continue with that regimen.' She asked him again if there was anything we could do. He said, 'I'm sorry. I must adhere to my medical protocols.' He said, 'What your son can do is follow his daily activities and maybe something will come back as far as physical movement was concerned.'

At the time, I could do little with my right side of my body. My leg muscles were rehabilitated to the fact I could maneuver from Point A to Point B but with a cane. My right arm and hand were just about useless. I could move my right arm negligible. My right hand was still a major problem. One doesn't know the importance of your left and right hand.

The fact one can reposition the angle of your hand through one's wrist and the ever so present 'fingers'. When you have 2 wrists and 10 fingers, left and right, you can do just about anything. However, when you're cut down to 1 left wrist and 5 left fingers, your ability to construct, assemble and fabricate is quite limited and impeded. Furthermore, my dominant side was my right side. I had less than a 50% probability to get things concluded and completed. When it was mandatory that I switch to making my left side dominate… it was quite a challenge. But I got pretty good at it after a year and beyond.

I always assumed the Lord put us on this planet with two sides to work with… your left and right side. When you're all of a sudden cut down to one side that's relevant as far as movement is concerned… everything becomes irrational.

But there's one element we have to consider… modification. My mentality had to come up with ways to alter, to adjust, to amend and to adapt to various situations presented to myself. The outside world was still having the same opportunities, but I had to confront them in a way not usual to traditional methods.

Example: You have to cut a ½ inch copper pipe. Now let me think… hardware tools come to mind holding the pipe steady. One could use a vise or vise grips to clamp the pipe down. Then, with your functional hand, cut the copper pipe with a hacksaw. There are many other ways you go about it, but this was an example.

All stroke patients have different issues to encompass. When you're in a similar condition like mine, you have to use your intellect to uncover the solution… modify, adapt and adjust.

And lastly… communication. The interaction and exchange of ideas, thoughts, concepts and such was in disarray. I knew what had been said to me, but I couldn't speak back. I'd have to formulate all the words in my mind for a response. When I thought I could produce an oratory retort… they had already moved on to the next intreat and/or question.

I was in quite a quandary.

We got in the car and travelled 3.7 miles to our home. My mother didn't say much. I looked at her and she appeared dejected and crestfallen. All I could think of was 'No more grueling and time-consuming physical therapy sessions! Yippee!' I knew what had happened to me. I was aware of my limitations. I thought the stroke was just a temporary setback in my life. Never in my wildest dreams did I think it could have so many implications and hurdles to leap over in later years!

HARD CHOICES

The EL Administrators 'passed' me from the Sophomore year at EL to the Junior term. I only missed 3 weeks of school, and they didn't hold me back which I thought the administrators may.

Dr. Reeve's gave me a choice or an option during July 1967. Dr. Reeves offered me to travel to Pennsylvania to attend a high school focused on handicapped individuals. Still at that time I didn't think of myself as handicapped, destitute, under-privileged and/or crippled. I thought about it for about a week at the end of June 1967.

Some of the things that came under consideration were a new living environment, making new friends and the toll both emotionally and physically it would have on me, myself and I. I was very fragile and vulnerable at that time. Emotionally, since I wouldn't have the support of my parents and physically... all those grueling exercises and training I would have to accomplish. Considering all these options, I thought the health issue was an interlude in my life. I could and would get through it by doing mundane tasks. I had no problem with that. I told my Mom and Dad I didn't want to go to Pennsylvania, and I would finish my high school at EL. They were elated!

I had quite a time that summer brooding over my physical movements… what I could do and what I couldn't do. It was sort of like 'Yes' and 'No' but it related to subjective matters and objective matters, respectively. I still had intellectual and perceptiveness issues. The most crucial element I still had, and it never left me was… choice. There was a saying in Hamlet that goes something like this, '…to be or not to be__that is the question?' But I had all the answers so to speak. I just couldn't say them. I wish my parents, relatives and friends could know what was on my mind… but when a person can't talk, he/she is kind of in a creek without a paddle and attempting to go upstream!

The first thing on my mind was Maine Music Camp. Two weeks in August the best musicians in the State of Maine from area High Schools were congregated and recognized at Farmington State College in Farmington ME for 2 weeks. I was going to be a first-rate clarinet player. I couldn't even read musical notes! Also, a clarinet needs 2 hands in which to make melodious sounds come through the bell. When has one hand to work with it's illogical to even contemplate playing any type of reed instrument. There was nothing to play except the brass instruments since they traditionally three keys to make musical notes. I had to tell my mother through impaired language to cancel my interlude at MMC. As far as my sister Pam went, she sang in the chorus.

I cancelled that year at MMC. A choice made and it was a heartbreaker! It had to be done.

Another choice was regret and disenchantment. It had to be this way. My girlfriend, Nancy Chesley. I broke up with her. At that time during the 1960's, a young man would give something of value to a young girl to say that the girl belonged to him. In other words,… they were going 'steady'. I had a masculine silver ring with a blue artifact in the center. She accepted the last of April of 1967. Nanc' had to put some gray yarn in the shank base to make it fit securely to her finger.

She was loving, faithful and a joy to be around. None of my school mates actually understands if another school mate has a stroke… it changes and alters the approach he/she reacts with society. Everybody thought I would be the same Jim. I was an anonymous Jim. It put me in a defensive shell. Trying to acknowledge what had happened to me and just groping and longing for someone to hold me and say, 'There, there, there… everything is going to be alright!!?' Never happened. I was still a growing boy.

My mother had a concurrence with Nancy during the summer of 1967. Two or three times a week I would call up Nancy and we would talk. And we would do what??? Talk!??? My mother said, 'Yes, talk, dialogue, converse on the events of the day!?' I thought to myself I could probably say 'Yes and No', maybe. This was a horrible idea! Nancy was presenting me with all these questions. I would think about Question A. I could respond to her in a few words (a sentence so to speak). By the time I was ready to reply and fashion my tongue around all the words I could pronounce to Question A ---She had already gone on to Question B! Frustrating!! Consequently, I ended up not talking to her anymore and it eventually led to a breakup in the first week of high school.

The first week of high school and the weeks, months and years to follow, I was just trying to navigate through the school building and life. Attempting to open up my school locker… endeavoring to get my combination padlock open and locked on my locker… bungling through my scholastic books… all with one hand! Not two hands which I was so accustomed to! Never mind limping to my next class with a brace on my leg and struggling to appear like a normal Junior young-man should look like in high school!

It happened on the first Friday after school began. After the last bell rang that signified school was concluded for the day, I was making my way down through the hallways. I was just opening the door through the schools operating center with didactic books in my right arm when I heard in an enthusiastic voice, 'Jim, Jim… Jim!' I knew exactly who it was and turned to her… it was Nanc!

I hadn't tried to avoid her. I walked through the halls between classes to travel to my next class, always on the lookout for her. I don't believe we ever crossed paths. I said to myself, 'Darn!' or 'Where is she!' or 'Maybe it was meant to be this way.'

I realize I should have gone up to her home room before classes began for the day and just be with her. But at the time, I just couldn't. I was scared. I was distraught. I didn't have absolute control of my muscularity on my right-side. I didn't want to be embarrassed and humiliated by my right-arm going up (it would be similar to a NAZI salute as I walked into her home-room). My right leg would stiffen up and I would amble into her home room like a young man with a wooden leg. I tried to concentrate and focus on the various functions of my muscle mass, but it just seemed to make it worse. I was thankful to the Lord for giving me some control over my body to just get up and walk around and appreciate life.

All I could think about was myself. I thought of how I used to handle myself and what I had become. I imagined sauntering through the hallways and everybody looking at me and saying to themselves, 'What's his problem??' I abhorred that type of recognition.... I was extremely self-conscious.

Nanc' caught me just when I was going through a hallway door. I was exasperated anyway since I was carrying books for weekend homework, trying to maneuver myself though and with the door and the congestion of students was bad enough. In consequence, when I heard my name and who called, I turned around. I said, 'Hi Nanc'!' She said, 'Do you want this ring or not?' Just like that. If I took the ring it meant that we broke up. If I told to keep it and we'll talk… we were still going steady. She held it out in the palm of her hand. I looked at the ring. Then, I looked at her. She had a concerned and loving glow on her endearing face. I looked at the ring once more and took it from her. She just turned around and went in the opposite direction.

All I could think of was 'no more girls.' That see-saw complication and obstacle was out of the way. I just couldn't deal with it at this time and with all the psychological implications. I had enough apprehension with my classes and just trying to get around in everyday life.

No one knows what I had to go through to conquer these individual issues. No one knows except me. I'm not being arrogant. It's just the way 'the ONE' intended it. Other ischemic stroke survivors have different concerns than I. Some survivors lose the use of their left hand. Others procure just aphasia. And still others lose movement on their right front toe and suffer with alexia… so many issues to overcome.

FIRST DAY MY JUNIOR YEAR

I'd been thinking about it for almost a week… the first day of my Junior year. Who was I going to meet? Where was my homeroom going to be? If I was going to see Nancy or not? Where was I going to 'make an entrance' to Edward Little High School? How was I going to carry my books into school? All these thoughts and emotions were going through my mind!

As long as I had it all planned out and I knew… and I'll repeat that… I knew what I would be doing in advance… I thought I could handle it.

My mother took me to school on the first day. I had it all planned out. I didn't tell anybody but I was going to go into school via the side entrance. I didn't want anyone to see my hobbled gate.

When Mom drove up to school she stopped at the front entrance. I said, 'No… I want to be dropped off there!' And I pointed to the side access to school. Mom said, 'No, you're going into the main lobby!' I pleaded with her!

Cars were beginning to pile up in back of us. Horns started blaring! Reluctantly, I got out of the car and shuffled my way up to the front door. I waited for someone to go into school and open the front door. I couldn't do that much since I was carrying my school paraphernalia with my left arm and hand. My right arm was useless!

Finally, someone came and opened up the front door. Whew… I still had another 6 ½ hours of school to go. Standing in the front lobby was my best friend, Tom Rowe! I was happy to see him and he was delighted to see me.

He put out his right hand to shake mine. I thought, 'What am I going to do in a situation like this?' This instance never came to mind when I was formulating my day.

I put down the articles I was carrying on the floor and shook hands with him utilizing my left hand... Awkward or what! Then, I had to pick up my books off the floor with my left arm and hand and continue to our homeroom.

One doesn't realize that picking up anything on the ground or floor with two hands is a synch. But doing the identical detail with one hand is quite a challenge.

The first bell rang and we were off to our first class. Trying to negotiate and maneuver through the hallways was a new experience for me. I managed.

My third class was English Literature. Mrs. Snow told us what she expected from us during the school year. Then, she had us write an essay on what our past summer was like. What we did and how we enjoyed ourselves. And she wanted the paper at the end of class!

I was stunned…

My being competent to read and write was just 3 weeks old. Through some revelation I attained it back! I had penned a few sentences down with my left hand and that was attainable. But she wanted an essay and we had to pass it in at the end of the period!

When we began writing I was traumatized. First, I couldn't write that well. Switching over from your dominant right side to your left side was daunting. Second, the only thing I could tell her was the reality that I was just trying to get back on my 2 feet once again.

I began writing. I told her briefly about my stroke. The fact that I went to physical therapy, speech therapy, psychologists, psychiatrists and psychoanalysts. A page and half later, I had my completed manuscript completed.

To look at it… all you could see was a mass of scribbly lines! What a mess and disarray!

I was relieved when the first day of school was over.

The next day in English class, we received the dissertation back and it was graded! I received an A+! I couldn't believe it!

The two students who sat in front of me were laughing over their scores. They turned around and asked me what I received for a score. I showed them. Their faces dropped! One of them yanked the paper from my hands and he looked at it. He held it up in various positions in front of him and said, 'I can't even read it!!'

MR. SIMONS

About the 2nd week into the Fall semester my Junior year of 1967 Mr. Simons, our High School Band Director, wanted to have a meeting with me. Just me!! I was so apprehensive! I really didn't know what the meeting was all about. Formally, I was an exceptional clarinet player. Furthermore, I played the alto and bass clarinet plus the alto and bass saxophone. I tried the oboe at Maine Music Camp, but I didn't like the sensation it gave my lips. Sort of a 'buzzing' feeling. It's like a bumblebee attempting to take off between both lips! My favorite instrument was the bass clarinet. It gave such a soft, deep and mellow resonance.

The meeting came during my study period.

Mr. Simone had 2 chairs set up facing each other. We sat and he asked me if I was comfortable. I said, 'Yes.' Then he questioned me about my love of and for music. I said I really enjoyed it, but I can't do much about it now!? He said 'There is a way… the E Flat Brass Horn.'

He said it's meant to be played with your right hand. In other words, one operates the keys to make various notes with your right hand. But he said there's no reason why a left-handed person couldn't play it. Mr. Simone's demonstrated with an actual E Flat Horn the band had in its arsenal of musical instruments.

And if I liked it… Mr. Simon's said he would meet with the High School Finance Committee to see if the school would purchase a French Horn which must be played with your left hand.

I said, 'Great… when do we start?'

Another issue arose in playing the E Flat Horn. I was proficient with a 'reed' instrument. That's what a clarinet is… a reed instrument. Playing the E Flat Horn was a brass instrument. One has to place one's lips in a different position in order to oblige the instrument to produce sound. Also, no one considered and understood the right-hand facial muscles and tongue were compromised with the stroke. It was a double whammy for me to overcome!

I started practicing with Mr. Simon's twice a week. About one month earlier I couldn't read, interpret and/or decipher anything written down on paper including music! I was extremely thankful for the Lord above in what he reestablished for me. I knew the music and how it was composed, and I was ready to perform.

About a month and a half of preparation Mr. Simon's said, 'I think you're ready to sit with the band and make music.' I was overjoyed!

It was December 1967and was the first time Edward Little High School Band had a Christmas Concert with me in the band. It was quite different from in the past. I would either be carrying a clarinet or bass clarinet to my assigned seat, but this time… it was with an E Flat Brass Horn! This was the first time my parents, my grandparents on the Hakala side, and my sister, Pam, could observe and listen to me playing an instrument foreign to their ears. Nervous or what! But I was proud to be exhibiting my skills in music!

After the concert, I went up to them and asked one and all of them if they could hear me playing. They said, 'Of course we could!' I think it was a little white lie, but I was beaming from ear to ear!

Just after the New Year, 1968, I was informed by Mr. Simons Edward Little (EL) had just acquired a French Horn authorized by the Finance Committee. I switched instruments from the E Flat Brass Horn to the French Horn. There wasn't much difference in the functioning of your lips. The brass mouthpiece was more defined and smaller but there were 2 or 3 notes which had to be keyed to a different format. Other than that, I was off to the races!

I went to Maine Music Camp in August 1968. That was a real adventure and a half! I was a French Horn Player. A far cry from a Clarinetist which I've done in the past.

Tom Rowe was there too and aided me with anything I needed help with. Mostly, it was getting dressed in the morning, helping me with my food (one can't cut a steak very well with one hand) and carrying my tray to the mess table since we ate cafeteria style. You don't know how embarrassing and humbling that was. I didn't want to be looked at in that manner. Other than that, I was pretty well on my own. I could say a few words and short sentences but always thought I was being left out, abandoned and put out to pasture.

I still had the same friends, but they seemed distant and furlong. I wanted to do the same things I did in the past that they were doing but I couldn't. I still had to get ahold of myself… the new me. I was in the mode that all of us upright beings have to go through once in a while throughout life… grief. There are seven stages of grief, but I'll spare one the tedium. The undertakings were much different from past Maine Music Camp experiences.

Once I felt alive and flawless! There was hope in the air! And the world was out there just waiting for my grasp!

Now I was passive. Just yearning to make it to another day! Knowing of my physical limitations and how I could best persevere.

There was a glimmer of the past and present… a glimmer of hope. Of all the imperfections I had to overcome, there was one thing in this glorious life that gives us faith and enchantment… music! Music to fill the soul, melodies to fill the air around us, music to harmonize with others and a tune to refresh a forgotten Spirit.

LICENSE

Driving a vehicle is important and essential to my verve since transportation is my livelihood. I have been a US Mail contractor for the USPS ever since 1976 and driving and managing vehicles is my profession.

Three weeks before my driving license exam I had my ischemic stroke. My father had to call up the BMV (Bureau of Motor Vehicles) to postpone my examination date which was June 12, 1967.

Incidentally, my father began transporting mail in 1962. It's a good occupation but not many people know about it. Thus, driving a vehicle was inherent and distinctive in my nature.

Dad took me out several times after my stroke and when he thought I could possibly pass the driving test, he made another telephone call to the BMV. Dad made another test date for my driver's license on October 20, 1967. Time was of the essence because my driver's permit ran out sometime in December 1967

It was the end of September or first of October 1967. I was out practicing with a Green 1966 Pontiac Tempest, Automatic transmission, 326 cc., V-8 on my Maine Drivers Permit with my father. It was rare in those days to drive around in that type of vehicle that had an automatic transmission. A majority of the vehicles put out of the manufacturing plant were standard or manual transmissions.

The obstacle with that you had to have 2 legs and 2 feet in order to drive a standard. I had learned how to drive a standard transmission before I had my ischemic stroke. But in this instance, I assumed I could do much better with an automatic transmission. Since with a standard you have two feet working below the steering wheel. Moreover, with an automatic transmission one only had one leg working below the steering wheel. I could bring my attention to driving versus fumbling around with two legs attempting to hit the clutch and brakes and then to the accelerator pedal to speed up the car.

I knew the conception and thought that went behind it. I could think straight and solve issues on a day-to-day basis, but I couldn't communicate or converse with family, friends and associates. Thus, in my life way back then, I was considered by others as 'deaf and dumb'. Just a paranoia I picked up along the way to my new individuality.

Getting back to the point, I was driving up Minot Avenue in Auburn Maine with my father sitting right beside me in the front passenger's seat. He was trying to train me to drive a vehicle with only one (1) side of my body fully functional. The speed limit was 35 mph. All my driving currently was done with my left hand. Through physical therapy I began to move my right arm just a bit. Thus, I reached up with my right arm and grappled with my right hand on to the bottom of the steering wheel. I was still holding the steering wheel with my left arm. I let go of the steering wheel with my left hand… and I began driving with my right hand for 3 – 5 seconds. I said to my father, 'See Dad… I'm driving with only my right hand!!'.

It was a thrilling and electrifying moment. Even though it was for 5 seconds… it was one turning point to recovery. I really didn't know how many other 'turning points' lay in front of me. Just keep pushing on in this astonishing mortality called life.

Nevertheless, Mr. Cunningham was my Driving Examiner, October 20, 1967, at 9:00 AM. I later found out later that he was tough and inflexible when it came to giving first time licenses and the laws of the road.

We went around the course making left and right turns, various speed limits were imposed. But two (2) most difficult issues one had to accomplish was 1) Parallel Parking 2) Pulling over to side of a road… putting the car in park on the side of a hill… engaging your emergency brake… disengaging your emergency brake… putting the car in drive… and pulling out in traffic without going back an inch!

I achieved those two (2) issues with flying colors!

One detail though. The last 200 yards of the course my right leg started shaking in my leg brace. Not bad but it was noticeable to me and most importantly, Mr. Cunningham. Mr. Cunningham said, 'Are you nervous?' I said, 'Yes.' I thought for sure Mr. Cunningham would have failed me since the shaking incident was clearly on both our minds.

I parallel parked the car in front of the Bureau of Motor Vehicles (BMV) on Turner Street in Auburn ME. Mr. Cunningham checked several things on his clipboard. Then he turned around in the passenger's seat and looked right at me.

Mr. Cunningham said, 'I've got two (2) tips for you. 1) Get a suicide knob [a swivel knob one manually installs on a vehicle steering wheel to make the car easier to maneuver] 2) Brake with your left foot.

Then, Mr. Cunningham said, 'You got five dollars?' I said, 'You mean… I got my license?' Mr. Cunningham said, 'Congratulations!' I said, 'I haven't but I think my father does.'

I hobbled over to my father's car and said, 'Dad! I got my license! Have you got five dollars?!' He was dozing in the car seeing he got up 3:00 AM to deliver the mail up to West Bethel ME.

We went into the BMV and made out some forms to affirm my Maine Driver's License. My father gave me permission to drive the car to Edward Little High School to resume my classes for the rest of the day.

After school was finished, I took Pam, my sister, and Diane Macomber home. It wasn't far… about 3 miles… but it was a thrill of a lifetime!

TIM POND

In my junior year at Edward Little High School, my father thought that he was losing touch with me. Little did he know that I longed to utter 'something' but I just couldn't.

We did everything together. We worked on cars, pick-up trucks, went on errands and even a box truck (straight-job) he utilized to haul the mail. We even went fishing and hunting together… enjoyable times!

He got talking with an old friend, Mr. Springer, up on Paris Hill ME about his quandary. He happened to be husband of the Paris Hill Postmistress. Mr. Springer thought for a moment and said, 'Why don't you take him up to Tim Pond in Eustis ME. You'll get to restore your relationship with him there.'

Tim Pond is the only set of camps on this freshwater body. It's located 7 miles from the main roadway, Rt. 16. On the way in… it was a cow path! It was just at dusk and we saw 7 deer, 4 jack rabbits and 1 porcupine! I was so excited!

It's beautiful, serene and if you want to be with nature… that's the place to travel. Loons singing, deer and moose coming down to the water edge for a drink, the nuisance with bears and night-time scrimmage to the trash bins (sometimes). All the wildlife you could imagine.

Tim Ponds Camps had a large lodge in the center for dining with 6 or 7 sleeping cabins on both sides. The lodge encompassed a dining area where you 3 of the best meals, breakfast, lunch and dinner each day. It was also utilized as a place to get together after a big day of fly fishing. Yes… fly fishing for brook trout. They had a front porch with rocking chairs on it where you could rock the afternoon away, talk with other guests and reflect and wonder about who knows what.

My father and I grew up on casting and trolling… never fly fishing. It must have been quite a sight observing my father and I trying to get a handle on casting a fly over our heads several times and having it drop gently on the surface of the water. But as the years passed, we got better at it.

The sense of being there was catching brook trout. But we had a great time doing other things, too. Like eating brook trout for our breakfast, we caught the night before. Talking to other fly fisherman at surrounding dining tables (and you know the tales that some of them say)!

I can reminisce when we got talking to a father and son at their dining table and their interest in the card game 'bridge' came up. My father and I both loved the game of bridge. They challenged us to several games of bridge after the day was through. We accepted.

Bridge is usually accomplished utilizing four players… 2 on a team. With me… it was difficult holding the cards in your hand and drawing out cards from that hand to lay on the table.

What I did was procure a small box with a cover. I would then invert the cover and a small slit would appear in the box frame. I would place 13 cards within that slit so know no one else would see my cards. Plus, I could draw the cards on the individual play without any difficulty. When all 13 cards were totally played the game of bridge was over. We would count up our 'tricks' and proceed to the next game.

My father and I must have played about 14 hands of bridge that night with the duo from Massachusetts. We won about 12 hands compared to their 2. I guess the people from Maine aren't all from the boonies… are they.

Shuffling the cards is a different matter altogether.

Getting ready for bed at night is when you sincerely delve into some personal conversations. Dad told me of his relevant upbringings and how challenging and rewarding they were. He told me about high school, the time he experienced over in Italy during World War II and he even told me about the event he experienced with me the early years after the stroke.

We also got ready for the next day of fishing. Tying leaders onto our fly-fishing line and debating on the correct 'fly' to use on our next day's excursion out on the crystal blue water. Dad taught me how to tie a fishmen's knot with one hand. Now, it takes practice but repetition upon repetition one can accomplish any task at hand.

While we are on the subject of my father, Dad was born in Norway-Paris ME area. He was born to a couple of Finnish origin, Carl and Hannah Hakala, my grandparents. The Norway-Paris region of Maine was a magnet for people immigrating from Finland. All my grandparents spoke was Finnish in the early years of my father's development. On his first day of school, when he 5 years old, all he could speak was his first language, Finnish. My father always said he could speak 'English' quite fluently in 3 – 5 weeks.

Nevertheless, my father often said to me when I was recovering from the stroke after I conquered a certain physical disorder analogous to moving anything on my right side of my body, 'maaratietoisuus'.

When he first said it, I looked at him with bemusement. Dad said, 'That means in Finnish, 'determination'. I looked at him with deference. He respected me, and in turn, worshipped him.

My father and I had a stupendous time being with each other. My father did most of the talking since of my predicament and significant circumstance.

I couldn't parlay to my father that the closeness between us matured even stronger than before. I wanted to express the words and feelings I had for our rapport, but I wasn't capable at the time.

As the years past, my father and I took groups of fishermen up to Tim Pond. That personal conversation was left in the limelight but we certainly had a lot of fun with the other fishermen!

I SHOT A DEER

My father and I always enjoyed hunting for deer in the late Fall… the month of November to be precise.

We used to go to the local sand pit in Poland ME and target practice. First, I started out shooting a rifle, Winchester .22 when I was 12. Then, I graduated from that and went to a Winchester .30-30. A little more recoil when you fired at a target.

We used to go hunting with Eldon Small who was a neighbor of ours in Mechanic Falls ME. Eldon was a real good friend of my fathers and my father always enjoyed being around him. Now, he was a real hunter! Whenever he sniffed out a deer either by tracks or deer droppings, he was off to the races!

When I had my stroke… everything came to a halt. During the Fall of 1967, I still went hunting but with no firearm. Just the presence of me walking through the forest was enough to alarm a deer.

After my first time out hunting with Dad and Eldon, my father and I arrived home, and Mom was waiting anxiously to see how I did. We went into the house, and she asked, 'How did he do?' Dad said, 'No problem… no tripping or falling and he kept right up with us.'

One has to realize walking around with sneakers or shoes was a real problem for me at the time. That's why I had to wear a leg brace for shoring up my foot. But when you put on a boot on that is laced up over your ankle…

it gives much more support and makes your ankle inflexible to bending or twisting.

The late summer of 1968 I had a little more movement of my right arm. Dad and I went target practicing at that same old place… the sand pit at Poland ME. I was able to get the .30-30 firearm up to my right shoulder and somehow, place my right index finger on the trigger… and fire off a shot. Dad said, 'Looks like you'll be ready to go hunting this Fall.'

It was cold that day with snow on the ground. Eldon, Dad and I were hunting off from Brighton Hill Road in Minot ME. We hunted all morning and nothing of any consequence came up. Finally, the 3 of us got together and Eldon said, 'Well, I've got to go, or I'll be late my shift at Marcal Paper Mill.' Dad said, 'I think Jim and I will hunt out here for another hour or so and see what we can rustle up.' There were quite a few hunters around and my father thought they could drive some deer upon us.

We said our goodbyes. Dad told me to go up on the steep ridge and he would stay down here and see if any deer crossed our paths. I asked him if I was supposed to walk around or just stay in one place. He said, 'Stay in one place.'

I finally made it up to the top of the ridge in about 10 minutes. I found a good place to stand that I had a pretty good view of the surrounding area. It was cold and frigid, and I had to keep pounding my hands and my toes were getting cold. I said to myself, 'I can't wait to get into our car and warm up.

I was looking around and suddenly a deer came into view. I couldn't believe it! I took a second look, and it truly was a yearling. I raised my .30-30 Winchester… placed it firmly against my right shoulder… got my right index finger on the trigger… and fired.

At first, I thought I missed it since nothing was there in my sights… nothing. I walked 10 feet forward towards what I thought was a deer and sure enough… A deer was laying on the ground looking around with its eyes open as in a nice undisturbed day.

I yelled out to my father, 'I got one Dad, I got one!!'

In the meantime, when Dad heard the rifle go off, he thought I had shot myself in the foot! He ran up the ridge thinking the worst. When I finally saw him, I said, 'I got one, but I think it's still alive. Can you go over and check?'

He said, 'Wait until I catch my breath. It was a long run up that ridge…'

He came over to me and told me to stand there, and he went up to the deer and gently nudged its head with his foot. The deer's head cocked over to one side. The deer was dead. Initially, we could not see where I shot it. No blood or body fluids spatter anywhere!

My father cleaned out the deer and he had me drag it out of the woods. We roped it on top of the car and Dad looked at his wristwatch. He said, 'I think we've got enough time to go over and show Eldon and I will still have enough time to go on my route to West Bethel ME this afternoon.' Off we went!

We got over to Eldon's home and he was just finishing lunch before work. He came to the door and said as he was walking over to the car with my father, 'You got one. Where did you get it?' I was standing outside next to the car and Dad said, 'I didn't get it.' Eldon said, 'Then who got it?' Dad was stoking his pipe and looked over at me. Then, Eldon looked over at me. And I said, 'I did.'

Eldon's face dropped a mile! He started laughing and began slapping the top of the car as he rounded the car 3 times! On the second time in his roundabout, he stopped and stared at me. He began in laughter once more and slapped the top of the car. My father said, 'We've got to go so I can do my route this afternoon.'

As we left his driveway I looked back and saw Eldon walking back to his front door shaking his head. Eldon, and plus my father, couldn't believe it.

We arrived home and Mom was inside. Dad said, 'Why don't you get out of the car and wait here while I go and get your mother.

Mom came out with Dad, and she was all excited. She turned to Dad and said, 'Where did you get it?' Once more, Dad said, 'I didn't get it… Jim did.' She put her hands to her mouth, and I thought she was going to fall over! She said, 'Jim… Jim!?'

My parents were so proud of me. I felt gratified, too.

Incidentally, we brought the deer into the barn and hung it up to dry age the deer. Dry aging means you get the best flavor and seasoning of the venison. After we hung it, I could see where I shot it. The back of the head called the parietal lobe… a head shot.

When Dad went up kick it, he kicked the head over, so the shot was covered up. We couldn't see where I hit it.

For the next week and a half, I got calls, people stopping over at the house congratulating me. They really couldn't see how I did it. But… I did.

GRADUATION

I finally made it! It was the second week of June 1969… Graduation!

Graduation… Graduation… There was a little thing that didn't set to well to me. About a week before graduation the Administrators of EL High School had a high school assembly to honor all the top achievers for their Senior Year. There was the best in football, soccer and baseball player. There was the best to succeed in the general part of life. And there was the Music Award.

Rumors were out there that I was going to get it. I just sluffed it off and said Tom Rowe has it hands down.

Tom was in the Edward Little Chorus. He was a brilliant clarinet player. He played the banjo and he started his own band called the 'Chord Majority'. Later in years he would become an excellent composer and was a member of the musical group called the 'Schooner Fare'.

The day came and I contemplated staying away from school with a sickness excuse.

But I went.

The last period of the day was time set up for the assembly. There were enough chairs for the seniors placed on the gym floor. The sophomores and juniors sat in the stands surrounding the gym. There were 454 students graduating in the year of 1969. It seems like there were 51 rows of seats and I was in row number 49. I did not want to be called for the Music Award.

Mr. Saviagno, our principal, made all the announcements for the 1969 awards. He said four or five lines of achievements of the person receiving the award. Then, the Music Award announcement materialized.

He said, 'And the Music Award goes to James Hakala!' I couldn't believe it! I scooched down in my chair… tried to hide from everybody but it was no use. Milton Ferris, one of our trombone players, said, 'Go on Jim! Go up and get it!' What an excruciating walk! There I was hobbling, limping up the center aisle with my right foot in a brace no less. And try to keep my right hand and arm down when I still had no control of my refurbished muscles. There was hooting and hollering and clapping as I walked. When I finally got to the stairs to go up and except my award all the noise ceased.

And I thought to myself, 'They noticed what was apparently wrong with me. How am I ever going to make it back Row 49? Oh, woe is me!!'

I accepted the award and the steps back to the center aisle I took them one at a time… it was a slow process! When I finally began walking back Mr. Saviagno suddenly said some kind, contemplative words about me and my struggle to make it this far. One phrase he said sticks out to me. He said, 'Determination makes the man!' And then the whole congregation began clapping once more. Looking back, it was truly a reviving moment.

Mr. Simone told me that a majority of the people couldn't do it… switching from a reed instrument to a brass piece. They couldn't transform their lips and breathing apparatus to make the adaptation.

After the assembly was over, I thanked Mr. Simone's for the privilege to be a part of his musical assemble. And thanked Mr. Simone's for being my mentor in music. At least that's what I wanted to say. Most likely my words at that time just came out as 'Thanks'.

SELECTIVE SERVICE

I intended to volunteer for the Vietnam War, but I hobbled in with cane to the Selective Service in Lewiston ME. I wasn't actually using a cane, but my father wanted me to have one just to appear more handicapped.

They looked at me shuffling into the Selective Service registration office. I gave them a few brief commentaries like my name, address and Social Security #. I also told them I was recovering from a stroke. I assumed I would be going in for a physical. They wrote on the Registration card my classification – 4-F. They said, 'That's it… you can go now.' I was sort of confused on my way home. I thought I would be going through a physical and such.

I would ask Dad when he got home from work what Class Code 4-F meant. He was an MST. Sargent in the local Army Reserves. He'd know…

At supper that night I asked him. Dad said we'll talk about it after supper. After supper, we went into the living room and told me point blank. My father said, 'What classification 4-F means you don't have to serve in any military service. They scrubbed you on the list for service.' I said, 'Really?! I can't be a runner, type, file or etcetera for my country?' My Dad said, 'No you cannot…' That was it…

It's not like a war veteran who comes back with a missing appendage or PSTD. I have empathy for them because they gave their bodies and minds for the rights of this nation.

At least most of the military services members can still talk and carry on a conversation. They can ask their best friend for advice to get over this manifesto. And if he or she is truly a friend, he can offer some guidance.

Whereas with me, it was totally atypical. I had no idea this stroke was even looming on the horizon. The ischemic stroke revised three to five seconds of my life, and it was complete. The impairment has been executed.

MARQUETTE UNIVERSITY

During the Spring of 1969 I was deciding which college or university to declare. I applied to four (4) universities and colleges.

First of all, my dream and ambition were to become a professional architect. I loved to draw homes! I would be doing my homework from school for that day. I'd rationale to myself, after I finish the last subject, I could get to work on my drawings if I had nothing else going on. But this controlling phenomenon made me take a step back and perceive me being in a whole new different context.

About 3 to 4 months after the ischemic stroke I tried to hold a ruler with my right hand to draw a home. Obviously, I had to convert from my dominant right side to my left side being the prevalent. When I placed the ruler down to draw a straight line I couldn't keep it one place. The ruler or straight edge would go all over the place! I even tried a yard stick to see if I could have better control of it.

Back in the 1960's through 1980's, society didn't have all these drawing techniques that they have today like the CAD programming they have on computers. Thus, I had to contemplate another way to, basically, make a living. I was always good at mathematics. I wasn't an Einstein, per say, but always liked working with numbers. Computers were just beginning to make their headway in our way of life. Thus, at Marquette, I selected Business Administration with Computer Science being my major.

There were a few institutions of higher learning that offered this major. I got accepted in 2 out of the 4 academia's I applied to. I finally selected Marquette University in Milwaukee, Wisconsin since they had a major in 'Computer Science'.

I rendered that was outstanding since the psychologists and whoever said I wouldn't be able to go to a higher learning faculty and had to attend a community college. It was a difficult and emotional decision to make.

First, my parents attempted to persuade me to attend an in-state college. My father even offered me a brand-new car if I decided to go to in-state-college. I guess you could call me stubborn or tenacious. But my mind was made up. Marquette University… here I come!

Second of all, I would be leaving the protection, security and shelter of home. After the stroke I always had the backup of my parents, my sister and my loved ones around me. They would abruptly fill in, say what I wanted to say and/or do what I couldn't do. I would go out or participate at home in various gatherings and activities. I (most of the time) had someone to support and/or advocate with me. I was very self-conscious and self-aware of my quandary. It was a big step to take advancing to Marquette University in my current and amended life.

I can recall when the Edward Little High School Band had an exchange concert with Elliot High School Band. An exchange concert was when the band went to another high school on Friday… stayed individually during the night in the participant bands homes… and had a concert Saturday evening. My mother was emphatic that Tom Rowe be with me at all times since this was the first time I had been away from home overnight. Tom was excellent at seeing my needs were met. Even when it came down to dressing me! One doesn't know how embarrassing and awkward that was for me at 17.

A number of times my parents or my sister or close friends of mine would say things that I meant to say but I just couldn't. They seem to know my mind, so to speak, for me. I knew what I wanted to say but I just couldn't induce my tongue around the conjugation. Frustrating or what! I know in this circumstance; it just hampered my way to recovery of an aphasiac individual.

It wasn't until Marquette University when I had no one to back me up as far as language was concerned that I noticed an improvement in my speaking abilities.

Everyone including professors, students, retail shop owners and people went up to me and guess what… they asked me questions, requests for information and queries. To me… that presented a challenge to communicate with them. I had to formulate words and discuss a position with them. I didn't turn around and walk in the opposite direction. I didn't stare at them and acted like I was some sort of dummy. I confronted them and gave my best response in dialect.

When I came home for Thanksgiving 1969, my loved ones couldn't believe the progress I had made in communication. I seemed much more alert, prepared and observant in my actions as far as speech was concerned. I gave the impression I was another person. But then again, it was just me…

Moreover, all the people who were close to me were always catering to my wishes. I was concerned about me and the fact that I didn't want other people to observe me in my crippled infirmity. I was cognizant of that and who I was in the past and who and what I am now. I still had my normal day-to-day tenacities and vitalities, but I just couldn't perform with my muscles to accomplish the task at hand.

Personas would drop me off at a location where I envisaged so I wouldn't be seen by other people. I could never be an example since I thought so self-effacing and dismayed of myself. Walking down the hallways at high school to pass between classes I always had to follow someone. I could never be the forerunner. If somehow, I transpired to be in the lead, it induced me to become nervous and apprehensive. The muscles on my right-side were in 'my' control but when it came to the general population that was another scenario.

My right arm would fling up and my right leg would become laborious to manage… stiff… in other words. This trepidation happened then, and it happens now to some extent. But I'm in a much more disciplined control of muscle movements than I was back then.

I had to get away and witness what I could do for myself. I had to make sense if this new Jim could make it in this altered and amazing new existence. When one is reading this book by no means the new existence is your fault. It's my responsibility and accountability . It's my millstone to hammer out and make something of the gift which the Lord has made.

Marquette University went fine the first few weeks. It was demanding walking to different buildings on the college campus for classes. I had been accustomed to moving to different classes in one building through high school. But I managed and became more proficient at it as the semester rolled on. In the dormitory, one had to walk to the restroom to do your morning chores as taking a shower, going to the toilet, brushing your teeth or doing other bathing necessities.

I listened. I listened from my dorm room to observe and overhear if there was anyone in the hall walking. Walking, talking, laughing or any sound one made echoed in the hallway! When it was clear and I couldn't hear any audible sounds, I limped on my way to the bathroom to do my duties. I was always conscious of myself and my body. I didn't want to be seen by anyone! I was embarrassed and humiliated to have a crippled body like what I had. I still hadn't traveled over the mountain that said, 'Accept it… '

I had practically a third of my 1st Semester as a Freshman at Marquette finished when got a note in Calculus class to see my Guidance Counselor - ASAP. I called him up and made an appointment to converse on exactly 'what' I didn't know.

I entered his office, and we sat and talked for a few minutes. Then, he moved to the nitty-gritty. He said, 'I see you graduated from Edward Little High School in the top 25% of your class. Your SATs are pretty good.

You know there's over 16,000 students enrolled at Marquette. Guess how many signed up for your major in Computer Science?' I said, 'I'm not sure?' He said, 'Sixteen!' I'm afraid we'll have to cancel your major until there is more interest.'

I was shocked. I really couldn't believe it! On my way back to the dorm I contemplated my different options. I deliberated long and hard. To make a long story short, I decided to transfer to the University of Maine at Orono Maine.

I reflected to myself what I really valued and appreciated achieving? I really liked working outdoors. To be with the natural surroundings and all their possibilities. At the University of Maine, they had just a major… Bachelor of Science (BS) in Plant and Soil Science. I said to myself, 'They will never take this major away from me.' Since this is where and why we owe our total existence. The foundation, the soil, and the flora that we flourish on. One can't arrive at a more basic consequence and value than that.

It took plenty of study and understanding of just how the earth and our ecosystem works. You not only endure instruction on how to grow a tomato plant and all its ramifications… but you explore biochemistry, geology, physics, biology, botany, plant physiology and the natural environment at large.

During my 4 years of college, I was on the Soil Classification Team my Junior and Senior years. Furthermore, a group of us fellow students went on a weeklong trip to Finland. My grandfather's, Hakala, birthplace! The excursion was to observe the wood harvesting techniques the Finns developed which were light years ahead of us.

I took a special trip to visit relatives of my grandfather. I just visited with them for an afternoon. Moreover, I couldn't speak the language, but we had an interpreter which was a sign from heaven. We had coffee and pastries and had a delightful time. That showed the comradery we enjoyed between homelands.

Through my years at college, I matured and seasoned myself to the outside world. I learned how to adapt, rework, change and modify myself to the society present. In other words, I camouflaged and masqueraded myself to appear like everyone else. I felt like you. I comprehended like you. I had emotions like you. I just couldn't respond like you. It made me realize, life, as we know it, has a time limit. Only He knows. Hence, make every day like it was the last day you will spend on earth…

At Marquette University I had no one looking over me. No one made sure I was doing the suitable thing. I was alone… trying to cope… attempting to do the right thing. I could do what I wanted. I could go anywhere that I saw fit. My emotions were free!

Like… someone would tell me a joke. 'What is the difference between a virgin and a prostitute? Answer: A virgin uses Vaseline, and a prostitute uses Polygrip!' At Marquette I could laugh… I would laugh for hours! Whereas at home, if someone would say the same joke I would be shunned at, as if to say, 'You've got far better things to worry about! Don't smile at the joke… it's disgusting!' I knew the latter was true. However, it was the enjoyment of the moment the leads to happiness!

AMY-JO'S BIRTH

One day… I arrived home early from accomplishing one of my father's routes during July 1967. My father was home according to the cars in the driveway. I entered the house at 80 Manley Road, and everything was quiet. I yelled out, 'Is anyone home!?' Finally, I went upstairs, and my father was just coming out of the Master Bedroom.

He said, 'I was just taking a nap. You're got home early.' Both of us went downstairs and we talked for a while. Then, I said, 'Where's Mom? He said, 'She'll be down in a minute.'

Mom and Dad were very conservative on communication when it came to intimate interactions. My father and mother had made an oversight.

I was trying to get adjusted at Marquette University. Students had an individual mailbox in the front lobby. Every day I went and checked if I had got any mail from home. It usually was from my parents. Sometimes one of my aunt's or grandparents would write. One day I got a letter from my mother, the first of October 1967. It was a 3-page letter. I was reading through it, and she wrote 'I'm going to have a baby'. I said to myself, 'What??'

They found out the last of August 1967. They didn't tell me in person since they didn't want to distress me in departing to Marquette University.

There was a window of 17 years… not months… since my mother has had a little one. It was quite a shock, but I was so happy for them.

I came home from Marquette University in December 1967. My mother was showing, and I asked her what gender the baby was. She said, 'We'll see…' I suppose she wanted the baby to be a surprise as far as the gender was concerned.

The infant was born prematurely by a couple of weeks. It was a girl! My mother and father named her Amy Johanna Hakala. Hannah was my grandmother's first name on the Hakala side of the family.

My mother came home from the hospital without Amy, which was quite unique. Customarily, the mother and newborn come home together. Amy had to gain the required weight to make her deliverance from the hospital. When Amy did make it home… everyone around was overjoyed!

At the time, Pam was in her first semester at the University of Maine. I was travelling back and forth between Portland ME and Auburn ME attending Continuing Education courses for the University of Maine.

We really didn't have time to spend with our new addition to the family… our sister.

Pam and I were engaged for the next 3- or 4-years attending University of Maine at Orono ME from September until June. When I was home, I was occupied by working for my father transporting the US Mail. Likewise, Pam was on the go working doing pursuits making income for college. Before long, we both got married and had a family to think of and raise.

Thus, Amy-Jo grew up as basically… as an only child. Mom and Dad did a good job in raising her. All the concerns that parents go through in raising a child. All the joys, delights and wonders were there, too.

My mother and father both said that I was to commend on the birth of Amy.

But one never knows what the Lord has planned.

IMBIBING THE SPIRITS

But that little devil in me that had been suppressed for three years had arose! At Marquette I transpired into the drinking phase of life. About 10 of us guys (students) when down to a nightclub to see if we could get in one Friday night. The drinking age was 21 in Wisconsin, and we were only 18. But we heard through the grapevine, if you gave the bouncer at the door $5.00, he would get you in.

The pub had tables where you could sit and enjoy loud music playing from a DJ. They asked me if I wanted anything to drink and I shook my head and I said, 'Not for me!!'

I noticed as the night went on, they talked something like me. They could hardly get their words out and they talked with a slluuuur!

Furthermore, when they got up and walked around, they were stumbling, bumping into things and falling down on the floor. They came around two more times and asked me I wanted a drink and I obliging said, 'No.' I said to myself as I was looking at the tavern and the befuddled beings in it, 'Interesting!?' Thus, as the evening wore on, I leaned over to Tom Kane, my roommate, and asked how you went about ordering for everyone in our party? He told me.

I got up on my chair and yelled, 'A round for everyone in my party!!' I got cheers, slaps on the back and I felt like the most popular kid in the watering hole! I even had a Harvey Wallbanger (a vodka drink)! My father always had a cocktail after work, and it always was a vodka reconnection and concoction. They say, 'Do as the Roman's do!' And that 'Roman' that night was my father.

When I sipped the vodka concoction it was strong, raspy and I thought it was going to burn my esophagus down to nothing. But, after my 4th vodka cocktail, I was the hit of the party!

After we left the pub, the dorm was about 2 ½ miles away. I didn't think I would make it! I went to relieve myself a couple of times in the bushes in the center of Milwaukee. Moreover, I upchucked a couple of times before we arrived back at our dorm.

I realized that this was the way of socializing that I wanted to be around. Because all the drunkards were just like me! They couldn't talk straight… they were all over themselves in other words, the intoxicated peers couldn't walk a straight line… How little I knew back then…

My college years were uneventful. I graduated in June of 1973 with a BS in Plant and Soil Sciences at University of Maine. I went straight into my major working at Goodall's Tree and Landscape in Falmouth ME employed as a Garden Center specialist in the June 1973. I went out with other personnel spraying trees and shrubs, mowing lawns, landscaping and doing whatever needed to be done at my employ.

Then in August 1973, I received interaction from Medomak Valley High School, Waldoboro ME, the administration was searching for a Horticulturist to instruct in high school. I applied for the position and secured it for a one-year contract term. I instructed for one year and discovered that being a teacher was not my cup of tea!

Next, I was employed by Skillin's Greenhouse in Brunswick ME being employed as a greenhouse workhand. I worked for $1.72 per hour with no fringe benefits. It was a low paying job even in those times since was employed in the 'Agriculture' segment of the Maine vocation classification. But to continue in my major, I assumed, it would lead to better job opportunities in that field.

Little less than a year, I changed my employment to Twitchell's Greenhouse located in Oxford ME. I was employed as a 'waterer' to the various species of houseplants in 12 large greenhouses. I received $0.15 more per hour, and I was thrilled by the prospect.

During the three-year period, I was still working for my father transporting the U.S. Mail on weekends. Additionally, I was still drinking and having a good time. Going out to discos, bars and whoever sold cocktails of some sort.

In fact, I met my wife at the Heathwood Dance Hall in Lisbon ME in the Autumn of 1975. Her name was Arlene Lagasse. We went steady for a year and then tied the knot on October 4, 1976. We had two children together, Kevin and Nichole. They had a challenging and difficult time growing up that some children don't have to face. I'm not proud of the fact but my wife and I were alcoholics.

Arlene and went through various rough times and anguishes but not between us. It all hinged around having a good time and utterly, tipping the bottle. Furthermore, her overall health wasn't the best, either.

SELF-DISCIPLINED

13 years later after marriage, I was having my coffee one morning at our gambrel log home in Kennebunk ME. Without warning there was a knock at the door. I answered it and there was a priest standing on our front porch. I greeted him and he said he was just in the area and thought he would stop in for a visit. The priest was from Sabattus ME. Sabattus ME was the homestead of one of Arlene's sisters, Lorraine. Arlene knew right off what he was there for, but I didn't have any idea… I thought he was just there for a cordial social call.

I later found out that Arlene had given her sister, Lorraine, a phone call at 3:30 AM that morning! Later, I asked Lorraine what she called up about and she said, 'It was all mumbo-jumbos!' The Father was there for a family intervention.

The Father said he was once an alcoholic, but he broke the strangle hold. He said alcoholics are always aware of the time of day it is… always cognizant of work and when one could take a 'shot' per say. Constantly looking at their wristwatch and saying, 'Is it time yet??'

And then he said, 'There is a way out. There is a way to get sober. There's a certain place in Portland ME called the Smith House.' I was quite skeptical at the whole narrative given by the priest, but I said to myself, 'Well, what is the harm in calling up the telephone number the Father gave me. Nothing else has seemed to work. Maybe… just maybe… there is an answer… surrender…'

I called up the number and told them about my wife's and my aenigma. They said they could have a interview with us at 1:30 PM that afternoon! The reasoning by the medical field was alcoholics have such a fluid mind. If the medical specialists waited a day or two, Arlene and I could have readily changed our mindset. We attended the interview with 8 doctors, psychiatrist, nurses and counselors included. The end of the consultation came up with Arlene being an inpatient in Mercy Hospital, Portland ME, for 30 days and me being an outpatient for 30 days.

The reason I was an outpatient was since my children, Kevin and Nichole who were 13 and 12, respectively, needed parental care and to make income for the family during this challenging episode in my family's life.

SMITH HOUSE

Thus, on February 10, 1989, at 7:00 AM, my wife dropped me off at Westbrook Hospital in Westbrook ME to undergo detox with my suitcase in hand. I was there for a total of 3 days. Then, the next day, I commenced my residency as an outpatient at the Smith House. It was quite an undertaking!

I had to juggle being a U.S. Mail Contract proprietor and manager which meant scheduling the employees, making sure the trucks were running to their peak performance, payroll, plus, accomplishing the job physically on a particular route.

Besides, I had to plan all the meals for the family and arrange for a babysitter to be with Kevin and Nichole while I wasn't there. Along with weaving in times with my schedule, set up by Mercy Hospital, Portland ME to travel to visit Arlene.

I had to be at the Smith House every workday, Monday through Friday, for 4 weeks at 4:00 in the afternoon. The sessions would last for 2 – 3 hours. I presume all the sessions were about our past life experiences and what triggered our dependency on alcohol. Take all that into context… I had to attend 3 AA meetings per week and if one was lax on this agenda, he/she would be kicked out of the program at the Smith House. This had to continue after I graduated from the Smith House since I had follow-ups that you had to attend once a month for 3 months.

The day of my graduation from the Smith House was momentous! There were 14 members of my class, and we were energized and jubilant! Each person of my class was given an articulated speech by his/her therapist of encouragement and inspiration. When it came to my turn, I didn't think my counselor would ever hush.

All in all, she attributed my alcoholism to my ischemic stroke. She said I wanted to be like everyone else. The only way I could be like everyone else was to be around drunkards. That I had the focus to be like you, but it just couldn't be.

I didn't except her assessment at first. I thought it was a ploy to get to something far deeper… my genetic makeup since my father and grandfather on my mother's side were both alcoholics. A heredity type of thing. But through the years I finally yielded to the truth. You can do anything if your approach and your mind is set to it.

You wouldn't believe the transformation. It was like night and day! You were starting out in this life of ours, once again, fresh and anew. I will never forget the simple saying which was pounded into my head at AA, 'One day at a time…'

I called up my wife the day I was released from Westbrook Hospital. Arlene was going into St. Mary's Hospital as an inpatient for 30 days at noon time on the same day I was released! I just wanted to check up on her to see how she was doing and all the necessary coordination was in place. And to tell her how much I loved her.

Lorraine, her sister from Sabattus ME, answered the phone first. I said, 'Is Arlene around?' She said, 'Just a minute.' When Arlene finally reached the phone she said, 'Hello?' I said, 'Hi!! How are you? Is everything all set with the kids?' And she said, 'Who is this??' (I guess Lorraine and Arlene thought I was an employee looking for vehicle assistance.) I said, 'It's Jim!! Your husband!!!' My voice sounded strong, resolute and healthy! She couldn't believe it. She said, 'Jim!!? Is that really you?' I was perplexed and astonished. I did not know my power of speech had actually changed for the better! And I said, 'Of course it's me!!!?'

We talked for a few more minutes with her and Kevin and Nichole. I had to get off the phone since someone else on my end was waiting in line to use the telephone.

After I left Westbrook Hospital, I immediately went to the local florist on Congress Street, Portland ME…it was February 14, 1989, Valentine's Day! I ordered an exquisite bouquet of flowers for Arlene to be delivered to Mercy Hospital. It was a nice sentiment and touch for such a beautiful and lovely woman going through such difficult circumstances. In the long run, life would be better, but still, she and I had just touched the surface in our long road to recovery.

Going through the Smith House and beyond was and is such an exhilarating experience. You feel much more alert and focused on the present and future. Mind you, you still have memories of the past and what you have done wrong or right. But you're more intuitive, motivated and have a purpose in life. Not being helpless, dependent and at the mercy of beer, wine, alcohol and such. It is a different domain comparing the two lifestyles.

Being an alcoholic, you're destitute whereas being sober you're self-controlled and free. And being a recovering alcoholic is much more fruitful and enjoyable in the day-to-day endeavors. At least in my opinion.

One thing I'd like to mention is when I was looking over Kevin and Nichole for 30 days, the first week, all three of us went to Shaw's Supermarket to do a big grocery. Shaw's has every variety of food on the planet! The grocery store also had drinks of all kinds including alcohol… vodka… Arlene's and my favorite.

Shaw's had a whole aisle full of hard liquor.

I passed by the aisle and Nichole asked if I wanted my special type of vodka I customarily purchase. I said a quick, 'NO…' You don't realize what a draw…what an enticement… what a temptation…it was, not to travel up Aisle# 3 and just see what they had to get inebriated.

I was pushing the grocery cart, and my face flushed, my heart rate increased, and I was all in a flutter. My body temperature most likely went up, too…

at least 102.0-degree Fahrenheit! But as soon I pushed the grocery cart past the end of Aisle# 3, everything calmed down and we finished our shopping.

I thought to myself, 'Was I really addicted to vodka that bad?!' I couldn't let anything in my life as a human being ever do that again. Occasionally, I've had different thoughts about taking a drink since people have come up to me in the past and said, 'Boy, you were the life of the party last night!!!' I've heard through various people and organizations, including AA, that your second time around is worse than your first! I didn't want to risk life once more. I didn't want to take that chance. The endeavor to live this glorious life was too great.

The Lord gave humankind the ultimate in the earth's fruition…a brain. The right to think and rationalize of and for oneself. The privilege to make choices. To know what is good and bad and strive to live life by the former. One hears others say who have been through AA, the Twelve Steps and such, that they surrendered to the Higher Power. But nay, they have admitted and yielded to themselves. The Higher Power is you…

I've been 35 years… 8 months…and 2 days as a recovering alcoholic (sober)! Not too bad for an individual that wants to get the best and most of what life has to offer.

ARLENE

Arlene, my wife, was a trooper. She took everything in stride and attempted to make the best of it. Most of the things that affected her were wellbeing and medical condition.

Three years after we married, she felt a painful lump on her lower left breast. I thought she ought to have medical attention to decide what it was. So, she did.

In a weeks' time she went to see a gynecologist and he took a biopsy of the lump. And above that, he did a second biopsy of the same lump. All the while the doctor thought it was just a cyst. The two biopsies proved the lump to be breast cancer with a little progression to the lymph nodes.

Arlene went to the hospital immediately after the doctor's appointment and had a single mastectomy accomplished. She was only 29.

Once I found out about this, I called my mother right off and told her what the doctor said. Then I went to the hospital, St. Mary's General Hospital, and told Arlene about the diagnosis. We discussed all the different options and choices that were out there, which were not many. She asked me if she was the first person I talked to about her diagnosis. And said, 'I called my mother to take the kids, and I told her of the plight.' A mistake I would never make again! Arlene got so mad, and she started crying. I finally calmed her down and said, 'I would never do it again!'

She would be the first to know.

Arlene had reconstructive surgery performed and during this reconstructive surgery she had her other breast removed. Thus, she had a double mastectomy with two artificial breasts implanted. Arlene wanted to make sure the breast cancer would not erupt into her left breast. She went through chemotherapy and the after affects were as to be perceived. She vomited after each chemo treatment, loss of hair, loss of energy and fatigue and such. She had to go 5 years and Arlene would be 'labeled' as… cancer free. It was one case out of millions that she would be a 'statistic'.

Women are proud of their breasts. A woman may have small, medium, extra-large or 47½ DD breasts. The woman feels dignified and graceful about her breasts. In fact, that is one of the first things that men are drawn to…their breasts in courtship!

I just can't imagine or fathom a woman going through just a single mastectomy! It must be so crushing and humiliating to her immediate soul. Nevertheless, when it is a life and death situation… a woman has little choice. Because that is what the Lord made us for... to enjoy a wonderful and charismatic life.

Sure, we may move on through trials and tribulations but isn't it great to be one of the living! If only people could understand and comprehend its meaning.

I in turn, had to go through quite a few adjustments. Socially, no one would know Arlene had anything at all wrong with her. Her breasts were camouflaged and masked from anyone to see.

Me… it was a different story. I always had on the back of my mind, 'Is she alright?' Whether we were with other people or intimately. Once I reached over and touched her breasts and nipples. I asked Arlene if she could feel or sense anything when I touched them? I looked at her and she shook her head and Arlene said, 'No…not a thing.'

When you think of Arlene's situation, with no electric signals or resonating nerves going to the vicinity… I couldn't conceive of such a thing. Thus, I had to find other ways to excite and stimulate her in imminence and to make her feel she's wanted… and whole… and a woman.

Everything went fine for the next 2 or 3 years. The usual labors with a growing family. Holidays and celebrations we enjoyed with family and friends. Christmas Eve with Arlene's side of the family. And Christmas Day with our side of the family coveting to see what Santa brought them during the delightful, starry night!

After we finished unwrapping our presents, the family bundled up and went over to my side of the family…Bubba (the name given to my father from Kevin since that was the only word Kevin knew how to pronounce for 'grandfather') and Nanny's home. We reveled, tore open gifts and had a sumptuous meal of turkey and all the fixings!

Then, a floral shop came up for sale in Kennebunk ME. Arlene knew my passion…to watch things come to life and nurture them into a magnificent plant and flower.

We sold our place in North Yarmouth ME to raise a downpayment for the floral shop. While we were waiting for the business contract to finalize, we stayed in a motel located in Kennebunk ME for the time being. My accountant and I went to several loaning institutions, and we finally received financing. But the owner of the floral shop had had it and he reneged on the deal because it took too long to receive funding.

There we were stuck in a motel for about 3 months. The owner of the motel came over to my room the last of May 1983 and told me I had to be out by the end of June 1983… No if's, and's or but's. Thus, I went out and bought a 32' camping trailer from Call of the Wild in Oxford ME. Arlene and I and of course, Kevin and Nichole, lived in the temporary housing until our log home was assembled into a livable dwelling in Kennebunk ME.

The family dwelled there for a year and a half when Arlene began to experience back issues. She and I went to local chiropractors to try and alleviate the excruciating pain in her lower back. She did a formulation of back exercises to lessen the affliction but to no success. We finally went to a rheumatologist, and he had x-rays and an MRI done. Those tests showed that she had calcium deposits between her vertebrae. Arlene had a back operation to remove the calcium deposits during the Spring of 1988.

The day of the operation I went up to visit her. A was walking to her room through the hallway and I was almost floored! There she was walking through the hallway with a nurse attendant. I said, 'What are you doing up and around! Didn't you just have the operation?!' She gave a little grin and said, 'The doctor said I should be walking 3 hours after I recuperated in the recovery room. So, here I am!'

I was never so proud of her! That's my girl!

It was during the summer of 1989, and we were both attempting to establish our feet back on the ground. It had been 5 months since our encounter with Smith House. Everything was going well as far as sobriety went. We started intimacy once more. It was awkward. It was inept. It was maladroit since we both didn't have that impression of spirits in or with us.

After 3 or 4 times of being intimate Arlene complained that she experienced pain in her vulva region every time we had sexual activity. We thought it was her dryness down in the region. It was no big deal. We tried it once or twice more but still the same was present. We decided to go to a gynecologist located at Southern Maine Medical Center. We sat down in his office, and he inquired all of Arlene's past medical history. He assumed through Arlene's medical history it was just a cyst. Thus, we scheduled a D&C and curettage procedure for mid-August 1989. The gynecologist said it should only take a half hour to complete. I waited in the waiting room when Arlene had the procedure done. When it became over an hour, I began to get anxious. Finally, the doctor called up the waiting room and wanted to speak to me personally. I assumed the gynecologist would talk to me and Arlene in her hospital room. I sat down in the gynecologist's office and spoke with the doctor.

He said there was a mass of little white pustules all over her ovary and surrounding organs. He said he scraped all the pustules he could get at, but he couldn't get them all. I said, 'What does that mean?' The doctor said, 'Your wife has ovarian cancer...' I was shocked! I never heard of the disease before! The gynecologist was taken back, too! I said, 'Comparing ovarian cancer to breast cancer, how would you assess it?' He said, 'Ovarian cancer is far graver than breast cancer.' I said, 'I see.' He said, 'I thought I would tell you first so you could tell your wife one on one.'

I promised I would call up Arlene's mother and her sister, Lorraine, as soon as I found out about the procedure and how it went. I lied. I had to because of the promise I made to Arlene when she had breast cancer. I told them everything went fine, and I had to go to visit Arlene.

I went into Arlene's room, and she appeared to be sleeping. I went over to her bed and brought up a chair. I held her hand and caressed her hand with my thumb. In about a minute or two she opened up her eyes and I said, 'How to you feel?' She said, 'Kind of sore down there but fine.' Then Arlene said, 'How did I make out?' I was still stunned by what the doctor told me. I attempted to tell her just what the doctor said. By the end of it I was crying when I told her she had ovarian cancer. But she was stoic and at peace. She said, 'We'll get through it!' Then she asked me the 'to-be' question, 'Was I the first??' I said, 'You were the first.'

Later, I met her mother and Lorraine the seriousness of Arlene's prognosis. Her mother came up to me and beat me with her fists on my chest. And she said, 'Why didn't you tell us? Why, why, why?' I said, 'Because Arlene and I made a promise together if anything serious happened. That me or her would be the first to know.' And it was just that.

The doctor eventually came in and asked how we were doing. He went into it in a little more detail. Before he left, he had an appointment set up with an oncologist for next week.

Come Tuesday, we went to see the oncologist. We had a long talk with him, and he explained just how things were going to be. Through the consultation, I asked him what 'stage' Arlene was in? At that time, there were 4 stages of cancer. One (1) being the less serious of the cancers and four (4) being the extreme class. He said that Arlene's condition was a Class 3 rating. At the end of our discourse, Arlene asked him what was the chance of survival in her particular class? The oncologist said, 'Not very good. 20% make it through to 5 years.' Arlene said 'Well… I guess I'll have to be within that 20%!' The doctor then said, 'That's the spirit!'

Arlene went through chemotherapy for 6 months. We had just sat down for dinner when Arlene got a telephone call from the doctor's office. Arlene was 'cancer-free' and she was in complete remission. I can't remember what we had for food that night but boy, was it good!

During this time period I had financial troubles. They were not caused by medical bills. That portion was all taken care of by health insurance. Two items stand out…1] being in the type of business I was in. 2] believing my accountant could solve everything.

During that time, I tried branching out into the insurance discipline. I became a registered member of A.L. Williams Insurance & Associates. I endeavored to generate a name for myself in the insurance industry, but it didn't work out. I also attempted evolving back into the horticultural field by opening a small landscaping establishment. That didn't work either with all the demands on my mind.

With all this, I wasn't keeping up on my mortgage payments. The bank tried to negotiate with me twice. Nevertheless, each time the bank came up to a higher mortgage payment per month than before. I knew what was coming next… mortgage forfeiture or foreclosure. Arlene and I discussed the problem, and we decided on moving back to the Auburn area considering the circumstances.

Arlene was still in remission but the oncologists at CMMC had confidence in if the ovarian cancer ever reared its head again. Plus, Arlene's parents, brothers and sisters (which she had 4 altogether) lived in Lewiston ME and my parents lived in Auburn ME. That was needed for encouragement, support and love. I finally found a home up for rent on outer Riverside Drive in Auburn ME.Suitably, we packed up all our belongings and moved from Kennebunk ME to Auburn ME in the late summer of 1990… just before school started.

ARLENE'S AWAKENING

Everything was going well. I kept my eye on Arlene as a protector and supporter . If any irritation or pain came from her lower abdomen region, I wanted to know about it, and naturally, it was concerning.

In the spring of 1991 Arlene was giving the hallway some painting touch-ups. She was on a small, wooden stepladder. When she got down from the stepladder she held onto her stomach and winced. I didn't say anything to her then since the kids were still up. Later, as we were getting ready for bed, I asked her about the happenstance. Arlene said she felt some discomfort and soreness coming from the stomach area. 'We'll keep our eye on it…', I said.

The hallway event took place on the first of the week. The coming Saturday, I had the windshield replaced on my car at about 9:30 AM at a garage on Minot Avenue in Auburn ME. While I was there, I received a call on the landline at the shop where my windshield was being changed. It was from Arlene. She said, 'It hurts so much! What do I do?' I said, 'What hurts?' I knew already but I had to ask. Arlene said, 'My tummy! What do I do?'

Arlene didn't have any prescribed pain medications and there was nothing in the house that could relieve pain. I said out of pure desperation, 'Do we have any ibuprofen?' Arlene said, 'I'll check… I'll be right back.' She checked and we did have an ibuprofen bottle. I said, 'Take 4 ibuprofen and that ought to relieve the pain somewhat.' She said, 'The ibuprofen directions say to take 2 every 8 hours?!' I said, 'Forget what the bottle says… take 4!!' She said, 'OK.'

When I got back home, I rushed into the house and found Arlene sitting on the dining room chair. I went up to her and asked her how she was feeling. She said, 'Much better. The pain is almost gone.' She took 4 ibuprofen every 6 hours and that kept the discomfort under control until we saw the oncologist the first of next week.

We saw the oncologist the following week. The prescribed Paula some pain medication and Paula had to go to the lab for an antigen CA-125 test. I assume if you take a CA-125 test done, if one is between 0 – 35 reading you're okay. Anything above 35 the oncologists take notice. Arlene's test came out to 78.

She went on an extensive chemo. Arlene had to go in twice a week for chemo and had the CA-125 tests done bi-weekly. At first, the chemo seemed to be doing a good job in that her CA-125 tests were reading on a downward scale. But then they started creeping up until the oncologist said that there wasn't a more powerful drug they could give her. Arlene's laboratory analysis for the CA-125 was 421. The Oncology Department booked an appointment at Brigham and Women's Hospital in Boston MA for us. We had high hopes since the oncologists mentioned a new experimental drug for chemotherapy called Taxol, that was showing good success in the fight on ovarian cancer.

We had an appointment and consulted with 3 oncologists. The last two said they had two recommendations for us. The first was a new technique in which they would do a bone transplant. I asked them how many cases they had done so far? They said, 'Four…' And then I questioned what their success rate was? They said, 'All four died…' I told them, 'It looks like we're not going down that path.' Their second piece of advice was…Taxol. We agreed with the oncologists that this is the way we wanted to proceed. They said it would take 3 or 4 weeks to acquire since the drug was novel and procedures and regulations they would have to follow.

Just as we began our trip back home, Arlene and I were famished! We stopped at a local McDonald's and had a bite to eat. We were both jubilant this trip had paid off. While we were outside on a modern and composite picnic table eating our lunch we noticed a payphone outside. Arlene had to call up my mother, Dawn Hakala. I thought that was kind of odd since why not her mother instead of mine. I said to myself, 'Whatever…'

Nevertheless, Arlene was overjoyed! She said they were going to introduce to her body a new miracle drug called Taxol. She told my mother, 'She wasn't finished yet and she was going to keep on plugging!' What a woman… what a fighter… what a companion… what a truly… best-friend and my love!

All went well for the next 2 months. The Taxol was attacking her ovarian cancer with gusto. The CA-125 levels were going down. But then, after 2 months, the CA-125 levels were slowly creeping up and then they took on with intensity. The oncologists couldn't increase the dosage since they were already at the maximum amount.

The first part of September 1992, Arlene had a colostomy. Our feelings and sentiment were twofold. 1) to extend her life by several months. 2) there might be a breakthrough in ovarian cancer research.

I remember the day of her operation.

I went outside CMMC for a breather. I went in CMMC and pressed the 'up' button on the elevator. And to my surprise Lorraine, Arlene's sister, was there. She was all in a panic since they just let Arlene out of surgery. Lorraine thought Arlene was on her deathbed. Arlene wanted to see me before she went into the recovery room. Lorraine and I stepped out of the elevator. We had to walk not to far and there was Arlene…

She must have had 21 tubes going to different parts her abdominal area and 5 I-V bags running down to her veins. Probably that's a little exaggerated but it sure appeared that way! I swiftly walked up to her and kissed her on the nose and said, 'How are you doing??' She nodded her head and slightly lifted up her arms to show me the conglomeration of tubes running in and out of her body. And I said, 'I can see. We'll talk after you get out of recovery.'

The next 4-5 months she got weaker and weaker. She tired easily and spent more time in the hospital bed provided by Androscoggin Home Health. We had a CPA coming over twice a week to take care of her personal needs and wonderful nurse, Sonja, provided from Androscoggin Home Health who came over 3 times a week who was proficient in hospice care. Sonja attempted to convince Arlene the best place to be was at Cloverleaf Manor located on Minot Avenue in Auburn ME since they had a Hospice Ward. Arlene was adamant that she was going to stay put and no one was going to take her out until her dying day. That's the way it played out…

The third day before her death I was doing everything to comfort and reassure her that everything was going to be alright. She didn't converse that much that day. In the past, I had been cleaning out her colostomy satchel whenever needed but nothing was coming out. A sign that her internal organs were shutting down. She knew it and I knew it. I had been feeding her 'Gerber's Baby Food' so her digestive system wouldn't have to work so hard. She could keep that down pretty well but if I gave her anything else she coughed up bile. During the evening, she wanted to have a last conversation with each individual child, Kevin and Nichole. Arlene had a short and concise conversation with each child… one-on-one. I never asked them what their mother said to them, and they never offered to tell me.

On the next to the last day, she didn't say or voice a thing. She gave different facial expressions but that's about it. Nichole and I were by her bedside talking to her, reading to her or giving her water when needed. My mother and sister, Pam, came visiting throughout the day. Her sister, Lorraine, and mother came over and spent a good part of the afternoon with her. Lorraine came up to me as they were getting ready to leave and said, 'She doesn't have much longer.' I yearned to say, 'Take it day by day…' But I don't know if the words came out or not.

Arlene passed away on February 19, 1993, at 9:00 PM.

It was my father's birthday of all things. It was approaching late afternoon. Arlene's mother and Lorraine were over at our home. Sonja, the hospice nurse visited a couple of times that day. On her last visit during the afternoon she said, 'If anything strange or unusual happens with Arlene… give me a call on my cellphone.' I stared at her and just nodded my head as to say, 'I'll do that.'

Lorraine was with Arlene in our bedroom about 5:30 in the evening. I was trying to prepare a quick meal for dinner. Suddenly, Lorraine came running through the hallway to the kitchen. She said to me with a large ladle in my hand, 'Arlene just convulsed her whole body!' Arlene had been fine that afternoon. She just laid there in stillness… closing her eyes at times… but her eyes seemed to be darting from place to place in our bedroom. I put down my spoon and went with Lorraine to the bedroom. There, Arlene was resting just as composed and peaceful as could be. I had a twin bed I acquired from Arlene's parents' house so I could be right next to Arlene when I was resting or sleeping and to be her.

I told Lorraine, 'Go in the kitchen and finish fixing supper and I'll lay here and hold her hand to distinguish if anything transpires.' I was there for about 15 minutes, caressing her hand with my left thumb, and an event happened.

Arlene's whole body shook and convulsed for about 10 seconds. During those 10 seconds, I leapt out of bed and watched her. This event was not a normal thing she does day in and day out. I quickly walked into the kitchen and dining area and told everyone to call up the relatives, friends and whoever to come to the house immediately. 'This is it!', I said. Everyone from Arlene's side came over except her father. Why? It probably brought emotions that he had been hiding for decades or he rarely lets them out.

Just in my mind's eye… he probably cried… he felt pain, and he was indignant. To see a daughter pass away before him. It's not supposed to happen this way.

I tried calling up Sonja, but she was on a grocery run getting food for her family. In 20 minutes, she called me back and I told her about the issue with Arlene. Sonja was there in 15 minutes, and she knew how to handle death experiences. Nichole and I were sitting by her bedside and Sonja was at times hovering above us giving us directions. Arlene had her eyes open through all of this. Nichole had the ingenious thought of giving ice chips to Arlene when she was thirsty or to wet her whistle, so to speak. Nichole and I took turns patting her forehead with a damp, cool cloth. Arlene would shake for 10-15 seconds and then was at peace for 5 seconds. Those 5 seconds were just like she wasn't there. Suddenly, she began breathing again. Arlene's convulsions and breathing became more labored over time. Sonja said Arlene wanted to stay here instead of going to heaven.

About 8:20 in the evening she had one of these episodes and she didn't begin breathing again. We got out of the way and Sonja went in with a stethoscope to listen to her heart. Sonja said, 'She's gone…I'm sorry.'

As Sonja was walking down the hallway towards the kitchen… Arlene revived to a living being again, a wholesome being and everyone in the bedroom was incredulous and astonished! And we said, 'Sonja, Sonja… she's back…she's back!!' Sonja rushed back and held a stethoscope to Arlene's heart. She looked up at me and said, 'She's back! She must be inconclusive about passing. She doesn't want to leave her loved one's here on earth.' Arlene was on a morphine machine, and it was giving a drip every 10 seconds to go down into her veins. Sonja told me that every time Arlene goes into this 'convulsive mode' for now on, press this manual 'button' for 5 seconds and that will give her an extra dosage of morphine to calm down the pain.

Personally, after it was through, I didn't know convulsions transpired into pain. I assume I had just hastened her passing.

When her life with us was almost over, Arlene said something to me. The first words and last thing she said all day. She was cognizant and aware of what was going on around her. I couldn't hear it well because of Arlene's low voice and all the activity around me. I tilted my head down closer to her and I said, 'What did you say, Arlene?' I had my ear right close to her lips and she said it again, 'I love you.' I couldn't believe it! I immediately straightened up and with tears streaming down my eyes, I looked right at her, and she looked at me, I said, 'I... Love…. You!!' with tears streaming down my cheeks. Through all this, Kevin, my son, was nowhere to be found. I found out later that evening from Nichole that Kevin was in the living room playing video games! He didn't want to witness the passing of his mother. Kevin told me there were too many people in the bedroom and he didn't want to be in the way. I don't really know the challenge or issue behind it entirely, but I know he loved her dearly.

She had so much faith in me, but I couldn't perform the impossible.

During the last couple of weeks of her life, I was frantically attempting to meet all her care needs. I wanted to make her just as comfortable as possible. We didn't have long talks or profound, heart-to-heart colloquies. But I can recall one thing she said to me. Arlene said, 'When I'm gone from this earth… get married again.' That was quite a strong statement coming from the one I love. All I did was look at her, and I said, 'We'll see…'

THE LOVE OF MY LIFE

After about 2 or 3 months when everything had calmed down to near normal without a wife and mother. I had just lost the love of my life and I felt so alone. I wasn't depressed, dejected or despondent. I still had a life to live. I had my two children to raise, and this was an ominous time in their livelihood to be without a mother… their teenage years. I got involved with a dating service.

I still had my work delivering the mail to keep me occupied. But still, there must be a woman out there that would accept me for whom I am and nurture our love for one another.

I had to do some paperwork which was about 27 ½ pages long and send it into a local address. Then, all I could do was wait for a reply with a woman's name, telephone number and a brief background, and then the rest was left up to me. I went for 2 or 3 trysts, and we weren't compatible, so to speak.

But then, I received the name of this divorced woman who had 3 children. Her name was Paula Louise Vienneau Wallingford. She graduated in the same class as my sister, Pam, at Edward Little High School in 1970. She had been divorced for 7 years and she was out looking for a soul mate the same as I. I was very nervous about calling up any woman to ask or inquire for a date when I haven't even met them. Nonetheless, I called her.

She was having a birthday party for her daughter, Elizabeth (Beth), who had just turned 13 when I called early one evening. All the revelries were playing basketball outside on the driveway except Paula, of course. I asked

Paula if I was interrupting something and she said, 'No, I wasn't…' We talked for a little while and she finally said, 'What extra-curricular activities where you involved at EL??' Talking over the phone right then, neither one of us knew who we were speaking to. I said, 'Well, let me see. I was involved in the Interact Club and, also, I was a member of Edward Little High School Band.' That hit a chord, no pun attended.

Paula said, 'I was a member of the band, too!' My little balloon had been popped! I said to myself, 'Oh darn! She remembers and all my hopes of a knight in shining armor are dashed!' I was taken aback, too. I said, 'What instrument did you play?' She said, 'The flute! Then she said, 'What instrument did you play?' I said, The French Horn!' In spite of everything that we've said that evening, we couldn't place each other.

Anyway, I asked her out for a date this coming weekend. She said, 'No can do… I've got plans for the weekend.' Then I said, 'What about the following weekend… say on Saturday, November 6, 1993?' Paula said, 'It's a date!'

Paula went over to a dear friend's house later on that evening and asked her if she still had a 1969 Edward Little Yearbook? She said she did and let Paula into her home. Paula scanned through pages until she finally found a picture of me. She said to her friend, 'I remember that guy…'

I was still wracking my brain to place Paula… and finally, I did!

It was that bombshell I saw at the Walton-Webster Junior High Exchange Concert practice at the Walton Junior High Gym. I observed Paula walking down the gymnasium floor, holding her flute, hips swaying, hair flicking graciously, her figure was like an hourglass and her face was picture perfect! I was seated with a clarinet in the band right next to Tom Rowe and said, 'Tom, Tom! Look at this knockout strutting down the floor carrying the flute!!' During band practice, I repeatedly kept looking over at her during practice and caught her eye once or twice looking over at me… my heartthrob!

This will be a little hard to explain, so, bear with me. The way Auburn ME was positioned as far as their education system was concerned was two (2) affiliations. One affiliation went to Lake Street School and the other group went to Central School grades Kindergarten through 6th grade. One graduated from 6th grade, and one progressed to another school of academia. The students at Park Street School went to Webster Junior High School while the students at Central School progressed to Walton Junior High School for grades 7th through 9th Grades. Finally, we all merged together as one big happy family during our high school years for grades 10 through 12 at Edward Little High School.

I assumed the 'bombshell' was in the same grade as I since she appeared old enough to be so. It was my sophomore year, and I was still a normal human male. The ischemic stroke was 8 months away.

When the first music practice for the Edward Little High School Band came, I was devastated since she didn't show up as I expected. I asked Tom Rowe if he had seen her and he said, 'Who… No… maybe she moved, or something happened?'

The next year she, Paula, showed up at band practice. All my dreams and aspirations were decapitated since I had one thing in mind… me. It sounds vain, pompous and arrogant. The ischemic stroke did a number on me. But when one could express 'Yes and No' with clarity and that was it. And you had to limp, shuffle and stumble wherever you went… indeed, you would be postulating, 'How am I ever going to get better? How am I going to restructure my life? How am I going to live an existence of purpose and meaning?' That was what was going through my mind. I knew what I was and who I am now. It's quite a leap into the unknown.

I can recall seeing Paula twice after I graduated from high school. Once was at college at the University of Maine. I was entering the Agriculture Complex at the university during 1971 and I looked back for some untold reason. There she was walking down the sidewalk next to one of the four greenhouses. Paula was holding her books (just like she did in high school) in front of her with both hands at waist level. I stopped and got out of the way of the melee passing to and from the building. I assumed Paula was going to make a turn and amble right by me. She didn't. Paula just continued walking in a straight line and sauntered past the edifice.

My heart was pounding! I discerned the day and time of my encounter with her. For the 3 weeks, no matter if I had a class or not, I waited in the same place, but my heartthrob never appeared again. I thought it was just an imagination.

The last time I saw her was 22 years later. I was waiting in line to be checked out at Hannaford's in Auburn ME. Arlene and my family were living on outer Riverside Drive in Auburn ME. I was coming back from LaVerdierre's Pharmacy after picking up some medication for Arlene's ovarian cancer. I was just standing there looking around at all the people, each and every one intent on arriving home and rustling up their meal.

There she was! Waiting in line 3 rows from me! I said to myself, 'I know that girl!? Where have I seen her before?' It finally dawned on me just before I entered our driveway. It was that girl again… Paula!'

At any rate, a couple of days before our date I went to Anne's Flower Shop in Auburn ME and bought Paula a beautiful bouquet of flowers. When I arrived at her home on Pinewood Drive for our date, she was so excited! The flowers arrived just about noon time. I put on the card accompanied the flowers, 'It's been 25 years since we've seen each other… I thought this would be a nice gesture!'

We went out to my car which was a 1986 Black Pontiac Grand Am and I opened the passenger door for her. Paula was quite overjoyed with this because I don't think she has had too many experiences like this before… a man opening a passengers car door for her!

We went out to have dinner at a suave restaurant on South Main Street in Auburn ME. When I parked the Grand Am I was so nervous. I thought to myself, 'How am I ever going to walk across the street to the restaurant with out tripping?' I opened up the Grand Am door for her… closed it… and we held hands all the way over to the restaurant! And I can remember Paula saying several times after… 'What big hands you've got!'

We had a great meal and after the meal was done, we went and saw a movie. I can't recall the name of the movie, but I do remember it was all in Chinese with English captions below it! I had recommendations from quite a few people to see this particular movie since they said it was a 'tear-jerker!' Paula and I didn't care since we were together!

I took her home after the movie. I was turning onto Hotel Road from Lake Street. I drive as I normally do and I had both hands off the steering wheel and steering the car with my knees. The reason I steer with my knees on occasion is since it's safer and prudent for me driving a vehicle. It's just another of form of modification and adeptness I've weathered into. Paula piped up and said, 'Would you put both hands on the steering wheel, please!' Embarrassed or what! I didn't know how the rendezvous went after that.

We entered her kitchen, and I said I had to get home to my children. She walked over to her refrigerator with her back turned to me... turned around and through her arms up in the air... came sver to me... and we both embraced and kissed!

And I said, 'I've got to go. Have a great rest of your night! Good night...' If truth be told, I didn't know what to make of the 'kiss'! Maybe it was a kiss that meant, 'I had a good time tonight... let's make it happen again!' That was the beginning. It's been 30 years since and is still going strong!

We got married at the Park Street Methodist Church on June 17, 1994! We went to Paris France for our honeymoon. One of the reasons was my sister, Pam, had a home over there. Pam got married to a dashing young gentleman she met at the University of Maine in Orono ME on December 30, 1974, to Wally Seymour. He was employed in Paris France working for IBM.

Paula and I saw the sights while we were over there like the Louvre, Versailles, a trip down the Seine on a riverboat, Notre Dame Cathedral and such. But boy... were we glad to be home and starting our life together with our new 'blended' family!

Paula took my teenage children, Kevin and Nichole, under her wings. She treated them as her own. It was difficult raising 3 children as a single parent and mother, but 5... an immense accomplishment!

Paula has always been by my side. Through all the dilemmas and delights. She's always been there encouraging, inspiring and reassuring me whatever I partake.

It's uncomprehensible to surmise what lies ahead of us. She's my best friend, companion, lover, confidant and my girl. We're soul mates through and through by this glorious Being through the Lord. We'll go through the rest of our lives hand-in-hand as we proceed through this breathtaking dominion called life.

CARBON MONOXIDE

The next 3 or 4 years were hectic! I was trying to fulfill my work obligations. Attempting to be a good Dad to not two but five children. There was Ian who was 18, Kevin who was 16, Nichole who was 15, Beth who was 14 and Amy who was 10. All teenagers, basically! It was quite a bit to handle! Simply put, I think in the long run it turned out just fine! I hope I was and still am a good Dad…

We were domiciled in a new home on 780 Garfield Road, Auburn ME. It was a modular home, and we had the cellar built into three bedrooms, a large family room, washroom plus a full bath. Paula and I got along great, but the children had a few issues from time to time.

It wasn't until 1998 the whole family got walloped by something unforeseen. We had the 'Great Ice Storm' that year. It happened around the winter holidays, and we were without electrical power for 12 days!

After 4 days with no electricity, I did some inquiring, and we purchased a generator over in Lewiston ME at Aubuchon's Hardware. When Paula and I arrived to pick up our generator it was a madhouse! The parking lot was full of vehicles honking their horns at one another… people were yelling and screaming at each other… and we even witnessed a fist fight or two! Were we glad to pull out of the parking lot with our new generator!

In the meantime, Amy, our baby daughter who was now 14, was adamant and insisted we purchase a Carbon Monoxide indicator. She saw too many factual stories of people succumbing to CO_2 during the ice storm!

We set the gasoline generator up in the garage since all our appliances… clothes dryer, range, water heater and furnace were operated by natural propane gas. One receives as a byproduct of burning propane gas…carbon monoxide. Everything went fine at our home until 6 weeks after we installed the CO2 detector.

I was loading bulk mail onto my truck off from Rodman Road, Auburn ME to travel on a route subsidized by my contract. The United States Post Office has a hub there to service all of Western Maine.

A mail handler came up to me and said I had a phone call. Mind you, it was 4:15 in the morning and you don't customarily receive phone calls at that time of day. I answered and it was Paula.

She was quite cool, calm and collected but she said, 'We have a problem. Amy came in and woke me up since she heard a constant 'beeping noise' coming from the kitchen. I went out to the kitchen, and it seems to be coming from the CO2 detector.' I thought for a split second and said to her, 'It's probably a false alarm or the CO2 detector is defective. Have you tried resetting it?' Paula said, 'No…just a second…' She reset it and the CO2 detector came back on with it's 'beeping' sound in around 20 seconds. Paula said, 'Do you hear that? What do I do now?' I said, 'Get the kids ready for school and I'll be home about 8:30 AM and see what we can do and where we should go from there.'

I got home around 8:30 AM and looked over the situation with Paula. It said on the instruction booklet if all else fails in troubleshooting the problem with the 'beeping' warning…call the fire department! Thus, that's what we did.

The Auburn Fire Department was over at our residence in less than 10 minutes. The department had three members of their squad combing the house for various leaks, emissions and connections to see if there was the issue. The fire fighters also opened up all the windows and exterior doors for ventilation. It took about 30 – 45 minutes to complete their inspection. The lieutenant came over to me and said everything was OK except for one aspect. We can't seem to find the CO2 outlet from the water heater.

Whether it is a gas stove, dryer or such one needs an outlet leading to the outside of a building to convey the CO_2 gas safely to the open air. I said, 'What??' The lieutenant said the same thing in a different fashion…no outlet for CO_2 gas to dissipate.

That meant that all the CO_2 gas coming from the hot water heater was being trapped in the interior of the home. The family had been chronically poisoned by carbon monoxide gas for 4 years! No wonder different family members had headaches, upset stomachs, diarrhea, nausea, mental confusion and/or fatigue in the past couple of years.

The paramedics took us over to the hospital, CMMC, and Paula and I went under pure oxygen therapy for about 1 to 2 hours. Our oxygen levels were stable, and we could go back to our residence. Meanwhile, the fire department had the house all clear of any residue from CO_2.

We brought a lawsuit against Modular Home Enterprise and the Gas Company where we purchased propane gas from. I remembered two of the workers coming up to me just before I, Kevin and Nichole, inhabited the dwelling. They said, 'We can't for the life of us discover where this 'vent' goes?'

It was a small 4" atmospheric vent designed for the water heater outlet. I looked at the contractors and didn't have any idea what I was looking at. Then they said, 'We've got a couple of more days hear and if we come across the 'vent' placement, we'll surely secure it in place.'

I discovered the vent in the garage when were going through the litigation for the trial. Paula and I settled out of court, and we won the lawsuit. But still, it's the dogma of the issue.

I was brought up a perfectly vibrant, healthy family that had been missing a husband and father for 7 years. All of us knowing we were going to have quite a bit to adjust and acclimate to. In consequence, I had to have them reside in this no-win situation.

We had a few health concerns a year or two after. Different carbon monoxide specialists told us that we would receive greater aftereffects and consequences years down the road. I ruminate I have overcome the effects well except my nocturnal myoclonus acts up once in a while. I've noticed the blended family who were there at the time have taken some legitimate, adverse turns through the years. Paula and I were always there to guide or advise them through it and remedy the situation.

Everything went well for the next several years. Meaning, we had our pokes and jabs that all kindred have. Whether it was economic, social, business and/or family happenings… we all have them. But the Lord gave us one item that most other living beings don't have and it's not laughter. It's the influential power of choice and what to do with it. I've fashioned some ill-conceived impulses throughout my life and there will probably be more. But I've made some beneficial commitments, too. Choice is the influential and dominant component in whatever one accomplishes in one's day-to-day actions. But one must acknowledge there's always going to be a consequence.

MOVING TO PARSONS ROAD

All of our children had moved on to college. There, Paula and I were living in a 3500 square foot home with nothing to fill it in 2004. We talked about moving to a smaller square foot home, downsizing, or building anew. We wanted to move somewhere around the Norway – South Paris area since one of my HCR contracts serviced that area.

I started doing research and phone calls to that area. I found a 3-acre lot located in Oxford ME, just outside the Norway – South Paris vicinity.

After my trip in that morning which finished in Norway ME, I headed out to look the property in Oxford ME through East Oxford Road in South Paris ME. After about a mile…I came to a screeching halt. I noticed a 'For Sale' sign on Parsons Road by Bearfoot Reality. I took a right onto Parsons Road and started down the dead-end road. Immediately, I saw another place for sale sign by BIZ Reality. It was a green Ranch and what a view! I slowly went by it and continued down the road since this wasn't the same 'For Sale' sign that was advertised on the roadway.

I found the house advertised but it was a split level. I quickly discounted that home since a split level was the first home I owned in North Yarmouth ME.

I turned around and went back to East Oxford Road. I slowed up as I passed the house for sale from BIZ Realty.

It was a smaller home than the one we lived in presently. It had an attached garage and even an inground swimming pool! I went by it and came to a halt. I put the car in reverse and backed up slowly. I thought to myself, 'This must be way out of our league as far as price is concerned.'

I continued to Oxford ME but never found the property they had for sale on the WEB page. I couldn't get the house I had seen out of my mind from BIZ Reality.

I got home and told Paula about it. We took a nap, and I got on the computer and found the house for sale by BIZ Reality. I was shocked at the price they wanted for it. It was much lower than I expected.

Subsequently, Paula and I got a car and drove up to the residence. Just before we arrived at the residence, I told Paula to look right. She looked right and all I could say was a look of astonishment came to her face. The view was spectacular! The mountains, the fields, the country setting and one can witness the Mount Washington summits!

We slowly went by the residence and there didn't seem to be anyone living there. We parked in the driveway and got out of the car. We walked around the residence. We took the stairs to the rear deck and just marveled at the view presented before us. We looked inside to the living room, and it was grandiosed with a wood burning fireplace.

Paula asked where BIZ Reality office was and I said, 'It is located about 2 miles from here.' We got in the car and drove right down to their office.

The owner, 'Biz', wasn't busy and drove us right up the property for sale. He gave us a full tour of the home and the rest is history. We sold our place on Garfield Road and moved to 17 Parsons Road, South Paris ME on December 12, 2004.

Since that time, we've gutted the interior and made it to our liking. When we bought the home, it had 4 bedrooms. We cut it down to 2 bedrooms. We rearranged the kitchen, dining and living room area into an open concept composition.

Furthermore, we eventually took off the light green siding (the only issue I didn't like about the house when we purchased it) and encased the structure with a soft tan siding. At the same time, we added a new roof and enlarged the attached garage so it could house 2 more vehicles.

One has the impression you're living in a country setting but you're only 1 ¼ miles from Market Square… the hub of the little town called South Paris ME.

SNOWBOARDING

One conformity I made to enhance my capability to my right leg was to propel myself down a ski slope. I could control my muscle movements with my left-side and that would be the side of my body that would take the most punishment. But managing the muscle movements on my right leg was an issue. I had still the same drive I had before my stroke. I was and still am focused and motivated by competitiveness.

Rick Grant, a buddy of mine in high school, he and his girlfriend wanted to take me skiing up to Mt. Abrams in Greenwood ME in 1974. We had such an enjoyable time skiing together a Lost Valley in Auburn ME before my stroke.

Presently, it was two to three years since the event and he and I have noticed quite a few of muscle(s) functions were coming back. So, I said, 'Why not give it a try!? I was very apprehensive. I went to Al's Sport Center in Lewiston ME and bought skis, poles, boots, ski pants and parka and hat combination.

The three of us went to Mt. Abram's Ski Resort in Lockes Mills ME one Saturday morning. I had no trouble walking around because ski boots are almost a 'brace' in itself. But when it came to skiing quite a long distance over flat surface to the beginner's trail or 'bunny-slope' so they called it… it was a different format.

When it came to pushing off with my ski poles to receive some momentum, my right hand continually kept coming off the right-hand ski pole. I hadn't attained the muscle group responsible to grasp the ski pole for an extended length of time. Rick and I went up the T-Bar together and had no issues. When we reached the top of the 'bunny slope' I looked down and saw what I was supposed to conquer. It was a small-scale slope versus the slopes I used to ski. I did find myself in a difficult position once I began skiing down the trail.

First, my right hand continually popped off my right-hand ski pole grasp. Second, my left ski was no problem, but my right ski literally 'wobbled' down the ski trail. Third, I couldn't even negotiate a simple right-hand snowplow turn.

I allowed Rick and his girlfriend to go off and ski on their own. I attempted to ski during the morning and part of the afternoon. My last trip down the slope was a calamitous one. I was halfway down the trail, and I kept looking in back of me to observe any other skiers coming down the slope because I didn't want to interfere with their skiing. I was embarrassed for even attempting skiing at that point. I caught through my peripheral vision an expert skier doing parallel skiing and having the time of his life. I had begun crossing the trail when he comes barreling right into me.

We both went flying in opposite directions. He got up and hurried over to me and asked if I was alright. I said, 'Yes…I think so!?' He was very apologetic, and I vowed that this was going to be last time skiing for a while.

Life caught up with me. I was busy raising a family and managing my business as a mail contractor.

One Sunday morning in 1977, I was watching television, and I noticed a novel winter sport coming onto the scene and it was called 'snowboarding'. Snowboarding down a mountain was something like skiing down a mountain.

The first difference was your balance. One had an altered and unusual equilibrium to deal with. Second, the snowboarding boots were quite similar to ski boots but it's where you put them on the plank or board. Ones two feet or snowboarding boots are all set, basically, in the middle of the board about 26" to 29" apart and your boots were angled to help with your stability. You clamp or strap them up like a normal ski boot but one's knees had to be slightly bent in order to maneuver around the trail. Third, one does not have any left or right skiing/snowboarding pole. One just goes down the trails 'naked' of anything in his/her hands!

Sure, he/she might wear gloves, if necessary, but you do not have a pole constantly in your hand.

Skiing down the 'bunny-slope' took a lot of concentration just to keep my hand on the right-hand pole leaving other skiing endeavors and struggles on the back burner. With snowboarding, I would be free of that aggravation.

It took about three decades when I finally per chanced snowboarding. I was 57 years old. There was one stop I made during the day on my work-related travels and that was at Greenwood ME. It was administrated by a woman clerk named Marsha Hilton. She was quite a skier and she went up to Sunday River. We conversed about the prospects of me enrolling in the Handicapped Ski Program that took place just after Christmas till April of the following year. I applied for the snowboarding program, and they accepted me! I was thrilled!

I arrived on the first day and they told me to bring nothing. The Handicapped Association had all the gear I could possibly want. The service technicians tried to find my size but a size 13 snowboarding boot was on my feet when I take a normal size 11. They stuffed some paper or cotton up the toe of my boot assuming that would help the slide of my foot in the boot(s). Next, they gave me an Ex-Large Snowboarding helmet that was too big for my head!

I know I have a big head… but really! The service technicians adjusted the helmet just as tight as they could get it without it flopping around on my head.

Then, they rolled a large hula-hoop from the handicapped service shop to the outside where the trails were. I said, 'Who is that for?' They said, 'It's for you.' I said, 'I won't always be using it, will I?' And said, 'We'll see…' They were disputing my competitiveness, and I viewed that as a discredit to my inner self.

The hula-hoop was about 8 – 10 times the size of a regular hula-hoop. They had 7- 8 men holding the hula-hoop up in the air spaced equidistant from each other. The dudes clasping the hula-hoop had snowboarding boots on and that was it. The instructor told me to get in the middle of the hula-hoop and start snowboarding down the slope. The hula-hoop was designed to avert me from making any sudden falls. I would go down 10 - 15 feet and the men where following me with the hula-hoop grasped in their hands.

It must have been comical to see me going down the hill endeavoring to snowboard with 8 men swarming around me! But I didn't care! I was having the time of my life! Maybe snowboarding was the thing I was missing in my life to strengthen and coalesce my right leg!I went to snowboarding classes once or twice a week. Each time I went to their sessions I got better and better. I was going up to the top of the mountain and snowboarding down on Sunday Rivers nice, smooth snow packed trails!

Three or four weeks after I started the handicapped program, I stopped in a snowboarding shop on way back for my lessons. I was motivated and thrilled about this new pursuit called snowboarding.

They had everything you could imagine for snowboarders. I purchased a snowboard, snowboarders' jacket, gloves and snowboarder's helmet. I even purchased a 'BOA' string system for my boots so it would be much easier to put on. As far as persuading the boots off my feet at the end of the day… that was another story! Sometimes it to two people to take my snowboarding boots off!

When I was tutored and took my lessons at Sunday River in snowboarding the instructors and volunteers couldn't believe it. When I fell down (which was quite often in the beginning) I quickly popped up and started snowboarding once again.

I was excited and encouraged to learn how to snowboard! My lessons took place in the morning from 9:00 till noon and the afternoon from about 1:00 to 3:30, the instructors and volunteers had a pre-lesson meeting from about 8:15 to 9:00. The director of the handicap program went over with her instructor's different points to consider on various aspirants in the program.

I was tickled when I was going up on the chairlift and seated right beside my instructor. He said, 'You know what they call you down at the prearranged meeting before our day starts?' I looked at him and said, 'What?' He said, 'The 'Energizer Bunny!' And I said, 'Why?' He said, 'You don't lose your vigor and you never give up!'

The 'Energizer Bunny' is a trademark for Eveready. The Energizer Bunny is a high-performance household battery which gives energy and potency like no other battery-operated device on the market. A bunny with a bass drum marching through a field or a downtown city… I was proud and humbled by the honor. It's true. I was falling down quite a bit at the beginning. I'd fall down on my butt, on my side and even go headfirst at times. But every time I fell, I would get up, brush the snow off my ski pants and coat and begin snowboarding again.

A majority of the handicapped participants when they fall down… slowly got up, brushed themselves off and peered down the mountain. They were contemplating what they did wrong. They were intimidated and/or they said to themselves, 'I have the rest of this slope to defeat'.

Defeat is not a word in my vocabulary! I was anxious to start snowboarding again. I knew the more snowboarding I could execute on different runs the better I would become! It goes back to the word(s) I realized and ascertained a long time ago… repetition, repetition, repetition!

This brings to mind the time when Ian, my son, and I went up to Sunday River. He was an invitee of the handicapped program. In order to participate in the program, one had to register for a one-day pass.

The inside lodge of the handicapped skiing program was all a buzz that morning. One of the past coaches/instructors of the program killed himself on the Sunday River slopes a few days prior. It seems as though he was skiing solo and he came to an icy patch on the trail. He lost control of his skis… flew off the trail… and slammed head on into a tree killing him instantly. A majority of the instructors and counselors knew him personally and they were heartbroken.

Anyway, I was proficient enough at snowboarding to invite my son to come and see how I was doing. Ian had the revolutionary type of skis that were shaped like a 'waddle board' which was supposed to give one a lot more control proceeding down a slope. A far cry from the ski equipment I used to put on and ski down the mountain.

Ian and I had a good time that morning… skiing and snowboarding at Sunday River. We went in for lunch and the Director of the Handicapped Program, Ms. Williams, came out and asked for volunteers to go skiing with her that afternoon.

I looked at Ian… then I looked at her and said, 'We'll go up with you!'

Ms. Williams had 10-12 skiing enthusiasts following her down a medium difficult slope(s) that afternoon.

On the last trip down the mountain, we were going from the left to the right of the slope practicing our turning like a zigzag formation. Ian was behind me and all of a sudden, I vanished from the group.

Ian yelled, 'Hold up! Jim just disappeared!'

What had happened was I was just coming to a turn and I turned too late. I went off the trail and down an embankment into the woods!

Ms. Williams came over to see what had happened. So did several other members of our group. But it was Ian who pulled me up and put me on the slope to begin snowboarding once again!

No more mishaps on the rest of the way down to the lodge. But it brought back recollections of just what happened to their longtime friend… the coach… especially, to Ms. Williams.

I can recall the Head Administrator of the Handicap Ski Program, Ms. Williams, called me up and asked me if I wanted to go to the Annual Skiers Association dinner at Lost Valley in Auburn ME. I would be attending the dinner with five (5) other handicapped skiers plus herself. I said, 'Yes…I'd really like to go!' She asked me what I would like for dinner. She said they have three (3) choices: 1) A roast beef entrée 2) a haddock plate 3) a chicken breast dinner. I said right off the bat, 'Roast Beef'. I later found out that she surmised that she would have to sit next to me in order to cut up my 'roast beef' so I could dine in a normalized fashion.

The event came and we had a great time! When it came to eating our meal for the evening, I took out my trusted 'rocker knife' in a sheath from my back pants pocket and began eating. Ms. Williams was sitting right next to me, and she was flabbergasted!

She asked me at the beginning of our meal if I wanted any help and I looked up at her in sort of an intriguing way and said, 'No… I'm doing fine.'

She had never seen an individual consuming their meal with a 'rocker knife'! What a 'rocker knife' signifies is a curved blade similar to a knife with three (3) prongs on the tip for gathering up food from your plate to ingest. All one has to do, let's say, in cutting through steak, is place the 'rocker knife' over that particular piece of steak one wants to eat, and start rocking (up and down) with your elbow. The 'rocker knife' slices through that steak with the least amount of effort!

I first got wind of it when I was going to Physical Therapy as an outpatient in the summer of 1967. The Physical Therapist said there is a way you can cut through steak using one hand. The Physical Therapist gave my mother a couple of entities to call and see if they sold 'rocker knives'.

My mother found a business located on Congress Street in Portland ME. Thus, we went there and viewed all their Physical Therapy equipment from wheelchairs, walkers to commodes! We bought two (2) 'rocker knives' since that entity was the only place in Maine that sold them!

When the evening came that day, we all sat down around the dining room table. We had 'steak' that night. I sat down with my rocker knife placed on the lefthand side of my plate. I began cutting my steak like a knife through warm butter. Truthfully, all of my family sitting at the table couldn't believe it! Me cutting through a firm substance and consuming it!

When I first began with the rocker knife, I cut my meat with the utensil… set it down on the table… picked up my fork… and ate the individual morsel. Eventually, I got so adept with my rocker knife that could eat the entire meal with my rocker knife! It was a source of independence for me to know that I could consume a meal with no assistance from others.

Nevertheless, getting back to snowboarding… I made a giant leap into the unknown. I envisaged I could do it. When one has the perception, he rationalizes the situation and goes on from there. And in my set of circumstances, I surmised I had the working muscles that could adapt to snowboarding. It turns out I was precise in my conviction. It's truly an exhilarating winter sport!

I had to bring the handicapped program to an end for two reasons: 1} My wife was doing an Express Mail Run in the afternoon. Somedays it got too icy and snowy I didn't want her to travel on the roads. And often enough times it would be on the same day as my snowboarding lesson. You know the next one in line to do the Express run… me. I had to cancel the lesson and go to work. 2} I had a fall in the Autumn. When I fall, (basically, I don't pick my right foot up enough so I stumble over things). I know through experience the correct way to fall. I fell on my left side to take the worse of the plunge. I was walking toward my house, and I tripped over something. I started to go down hard but my left shoulder and arm were there to soften the blow. When I got up, I noticed my left shoulder was in quite a bit of pain. I assume I had torn, strained and/or pulled my left rotator cuff. But being the strong, individualist person that I am, I didn't seek any medical treatment or therapy which I should have. It took 4 or 5 months for the shoulder to heal completely.

These two conflicts circumstanced my withdrawal from the handicapped program that year. And in years to come I haven't been snowboarding. I'm truly grateful for the instructors, volunteers, and characters taking part in the program, and I'm indebted to my wife for going along with it for so long.

CARPAL TUNNEL SYNDROME

About the same time in 2009, I began to notice my left hand. The only functional hand to do anything… like chores around the house, gardening, keeping up the lawn, eating, shoveling snow during the winter and most importantly… my vocation…a U.S. Mail contractor.

My left-hand began to go numb. Sometimes I couldn't feel a thing. One doesn't know what an appalling awareness that is. I would get shooting pains in my left wrist and hand from time to time. Furthermore, when you have one functional and purposeful arm and hand, my left torso appendage, you acquire concern over your life for the past 45 years and the imminent years ahead. I've made it this far… what am I supposed to accomplish with nothing to do and with the responsibilities I've had so far?

Amy Case, our youngest daughter paid a visit to our home during the spring. She is a practicing Physicians Assistant (PA) and knows quite a bit about the human body and its functions.

I complained about my left hand and how it went numb once in a while. Nonchalantly, she wanted to see my left-hand palm. I turned my left-hand palm over and she could see immediately the convex area below my left thumb. That was the area the median nerves inhabited and the median nerve travels right through the carpal tunnel ligament. She said, 'The next time you go to a doctor, mention your left-hand to her and discern what she says.

I went to visit Dr. Jett for my yearly physical a couple of weeks later. During the exam I asked her about my left-hand and the difficulties it's been exhibiting lately. She looked at my left-hand, turned it over a couple of times and said, 'I'll make a referral to a surgeon who specialized in carpal tunnel surgery, and he's located in Brunswick ME. I asked Dr. Jett if I could still continue to work. She said, 'I don't see why not.'

My wife and I had arrived home and put around doing our own separate things for a couple of hours when the phone rang. It was Dr. Jett. I took the phone and said, 'What's up???' Dr. Jett said, 'I told you earlier you could go back to work. Scratch that… I don't want you working or doing a thing until you see the specialist. OK?' I said, 'It can be arranged.'

I had my appointment down in Brunswick ME. During the visit the medical technician did various things to my left hand. He took me through the 'motions' so to speak. One test I can recall was a 'pin test'. He had me flip over my left hand, so my left palm was facing up. He had me close my eyes, so I was void of sight. The medical technician told me to tell him if I felt or sensed anything while he was performing this test. Then, he pricked my left palm about 15 times at various points. The test only took about 30 – 45 seconds. He told me to open my eyes. I looked at him, ready for the test to begin. He said, 'You're finished with this procedure.' I said, 'What?' I stared at him and then looked at my wife. I said, 'I didn't feel a thing!'

We asked the doctor if we could have a second opinion. He said, 'Sure. I'll see if I could make the appointment today.' An hour and half later we were sitting in another doctor's office, and I was told the same thing leading to 'carpal tunnel surgery'. The doctor said I overworked my left hand which led to my predicament. Again, I said, 'We would like a second opinion.' And the doctor said, 'I am the second opinion. There's no place else to go.'

The surgery lasted about an hour and a half. The doctor said, '100% recovery!' The recovery at home truly was a difficult time the first week and a half. I postulate an individual proceeding through recovery from carpal tunnel surgery would have a somewhat difficult time with 2 hands. But a person with 1 hand to utilize and that was the hand you had the carpal tunnel surgery achieved on… very problematic. I had to ask my wife to assist me in getting dressed no matter what time of day it was. My wife helped me when I had to go to the bathroom. I had to eat my meals by way of plastic utensils. If I ate with metal utensils it would cause aching in my left hand.

At random during the day, I had a dull, quelling pain going through my left lower arm and hand which lasted for about 30 – 45 seconds. That was captivating! But it got better day by day. At my last appointment at the doctor's office six weeks after the surgery he said I could resume daily chores around the house, and I was elated! My left hand felt much improved, but it still wasn't 100%. My left sensory median nerves were enhanced, and I was thankful.

But going back to work operating a 24' straight-job with a tuck-away tailgate lift was another matter. I had to reason I just had surgery on my only functional hand. I didn't want to jeopardize my hand in any way.

Basically, I just stayed at home and worked out of my home-office location. I applied myself as a general manager. I made sure all the trucks were in tip-top operating condition. I accomplished the weekly schedules and dispatched them when necessary. I communicated with the USPS from time to time to make sure everything from my end was running smoothly. Logistics is the key to anything in the transportation business. Especially between the HCR Contractor and Administrative Post Office Head of the USPS.No one told me… No one told me about carpal tunnel syndrome. It's the most disconcerting disorder that an individual could have, especially with one performing hand of a person who has relied upon my venerable left hand for 45 years.

Not any doctors, nurses, PA's or NP's, friends, therapists, masseurs, relatives, associates and/or acquaintances have even quipped about it. I was aware of carpal tunnel syndrome by different news broadcasts, but I thought it was related to the computer work force by typing on the keyboard!

I was utterly unaware until Amy stopped by for a social visit. I was in the dark until the syndrome reared its ugly head upon me. Perchance, I would have listened to anyone who raised this consequence. But again, I am a very stubborn and obstinate individual but optimistic at that. Most likely I would have sloughed it off and said, 'They don't know what they are talking about.'

Predominantly, one would utilize two hands on a keyboard to capture their concepts. One takes in my situation; I'm currently typing on my keyboard with my left hand. I've memorized the particular keys on my typing instrument. And I have a smaller keyboard to facilitate the use of it to a more comfortable application… inputting my thoughts on paper. But I must look down to observe I'm typing the correct keys since I have no feeling in my fingertips. It's bothersome, annoying and nettlesome. But then again, one can accomplish something even with the most tedious and interesting of pursuits through modification.

Everything went fine for the next several years. I denote my wife and I had family issues, loved one's passing away, issues with our business and other questions through this livelihood of ours.

But I still have my garden to care for every year. Whether it's a vegetable plot, a flower garden, taking care of my attractive lawn and nourishing my shrubs and trees… it's there just for my picking! All I can say is 'Joy to the World!' As I said in the beginning of this book 'they will never take this major away from me…BS in Plant and Soil Science.'

MYOPRO

It was the last of January 2022. I got up one night since I couldn't get to sleep because of my nocturnal myoclonus.

Nocturnal myoclonus is a syndrome that emerges at night just when you're supposed to go to sleep. Myoclonus is a twitching, jerking and/or jolting of one or more of your appendages. It usually occurs in a rhythmic cycle, like every 43 seconds. Moreover, it occurs just when you're ready to go off into a peaceful night's sleep.

The medical profession conjectures one of the explanations myoclonus is prevalent in some patients with a brain injury… or a stroke. I didn't notice it right after the stroke but I really was agitated with myoclonus after the carbon monoxide exposure.

Nonetheless, I came down in my office and started surfing the Web. I was looking for something entirely different when all of a sudden, this Web page came up… MyoPro. I looked at the caption and read it. I said to myself, 'Oomph… this isn't what I was looking for!' Thus, I began surfing for the specific subject I was looking for once again. Then… in a flash… this identical Web site popped up for a second time… MyoPro. I stared at it. I said, 'What in tarnation!?' I started to read the Web pages. I saw different 'videos' to explain what MyoPro could accomplish.

Essentially, it is for people who have suffered an ischemic stroke or have a medical condition affecting the brain involving the upper torso. I said to myself, 'I sounds like something just up my alley.' Furthermore, MyoPro is a 'robotic arm' which takes the electric isometric signals from the brain and amplifies them up to 100.000 times its original intensity.

My left hand is slowly deteriorating to the carpal tunnel syndrome once again. I assume I could assist my upper left side torso if I had a little more flexibility with my right side. I want to be like everyone else using their upper torso in a normal way. I long for it… even now… 56 years later!

Thus, I typed in the application online and sent it in. And to my surprise I got a callback the next day. It was from the Administrative Division with new clients. She was congenial and we talked for about 20 minutes. She asked about the stroke briefly. She asked me if I could reach the floor with my right hand and couple of more muscle movements. I did them hands down. She said you sound like a perfect candidate for MyoPro. Then she said, 'I will be receiving a call from Sarah who will go into this in more detail and take videos of different movements of myself as far as physical exertions are concerned.

Two days later I received an unexpected call from Sarah from MyoPro. She asked if I was free for the next hour and a half. I said, 'Sure… let's get into it!' The total time it encompassed was just short of three hours!

Sarah took me through all sorts of exercises on video or recording… things I wasn't accustomed to using my right upper toro, exclusively. She said I did good, and she wanted all medical records relating to my ischemic stroke. I didn't think that would be too hard. Just call up CMMC, Lewiston ME and ask for them in the archives department. I tried for 5 weeks to obtain physical documents related to my stroke… No Go. Come to find out, all hospitals in the State of Maine have it mandatory to destroy their documents and records 20 years out! With computers, tablets and/or thumb drives I didn't think anyone's data would be lost. Thus, I didn't have any chance of locating them since my ischemic stroke evolved 56 years ago.

I even called up Dr. Reeves son, Robert Reeves, who was 74 years old from Gardiner ME, if he had any old records or documents from Dr. Reeves practice on Sabattus Street, Lewiston ME. He is a retired lawyer so I thought… just maybe… he would have some old documents or notes. We had a long chat over the phone bringing back memorabilia of our generation. But no… he didn't have any accounts of Dr. Reeves actions. Mr. Reeves said he would ask his sister, who lived on the coast of Maine if she had any of his past medical records. I didn't hear from him again; therefore, I assume not.

Sarah said that customarily she fills 2 or 3 pages to submit to the client's health insurance entity. But with MyoPro, she has to acquiesce at least 28 pages to the health insurance concern.

Additionally, Sarah wanted a 'prescription' from my current primary physician, Dr. Inga Johansson, stating I needed this device to augment my recovery on my right upper torso. Dr. Johansson wrote a formal statement to Martins Point Health Insurer telling them of my limited movement on my right side. She also told my health insures the MyoPro was needed for my recovery to become somewhat of a normal man.

A month passed as I got a letter from Martin's Point stating the didn't see any reason why I should have it. In other words, they 'rejected' my application for the MyoPro.

Up until June 2022, I received two (2) more denials from Martin's Point. Every time I received one, I said, 'Reapply'. Eventually, in June 2022 MyoPro said that they had exhausted all resources to obtain a MyoPro but there is another avenue we could travel. An administrative law judge can hear your case over the telephone, and it will be recorded. He/she will lay down their decision no more than 2 weeks from your conference call. MyoPro said it will be no cost to me in that MyoPro will foot the bill. I said, 'Go for it.'

It was the end of June 2022. I received a call from Pittsburgh PA from a lawyer's office, Parrish Law Office. Debra Parrish was the lawyer who was going to be representing me in front of the Administrative Law Judge. In addition, the time and place had already been set for the telephone conference call, July 21, 2022, at 1:00 PM.

I had to prepare. I had to get my thoughts together.

The day came. The Administrative Judge, two prosecutors from MyoPro, two defendants from the health insurance provider and myself were on the tele-conference. All of them gave a rehearsed discourse. With me, it was just off the cuff. Assured, I had some notes written down and they were ordered. I really didn't know what to say since I had never been before with any type of judge ruling on my livelihood. Here's how it briefly went:

We all gave our introductions to who we were and our credentials. The prosecutors and defendant gave an entailed and luminous discourse. When the prosecutor(s) finished the judge asked me if I wanted to go next (I was nervous). I said let the defendant proceed next and I'll give the closing remarks. The defendant gave his interchange and next it was my turn.

I applauded and complimented the prosecutor(s) and defended(s) for their appraisals. They were detailed and I never heard anyone giving such a comprehensive narrative of traumatic brain injury and all the issues they had to consider.

I told them about the date my ischemic stroke happened. How my paralysis occurred on my dominant side. I had to relearn how to walk, talk, read and how I had aphasia and alexia. To overcome that peril was a feat in itself.

There were two (2) things I hoped to accomplish in my lifelong mêlée of being a stroke survivor. 1) to communicate… I said I think I've conquered that threshold. And I noticed a little laugh coming from the other end. 2) to utilize my right arm and hand so I can function with the appendage.

Furthermore, the one most important thing I've learned and realized is 'patience'.

To further my recovery of my right arm… I've been to physical and occupational therapy… I've pursued electrical stimulation… I've been to a chiropractor and message therapy. Countless rehab specialists have said to me that by doing normal activities on a day-to-day basis may encourage and convalesce movement in my right arm, leg and hand.

And of course, I did a lot of praying.

It was silent for a moment. And then the Administrative Judge spoke up and said, 'Well if that's it…' Then I said, 'If you don't mind… there's one more thing I would like say?' She said, 'Go ahead.'

Then I said, 'You don't know how awesome it would be…' (then, I broke up)'… to sit at a dining room table… and eat with two hands… That's it…'

It was silent for 3-5 seconds. And then the Administrative Judge said, 'Thank you for that emotional testimony! '

I didn't think it was an emotional testimony. It was the truth. I recognized and knew it was a proclamation coming from the heart and soul of my inner being. The things and occurrences I've been through… no one will ever understand but me.

There was a flurry of activity, and they all seemed enlivened asking for documents here and motions there.

The Administrative Judge said you'll receive my ruling in 2 – 3 weeks.

It was two weeks later when I received a letter through the mail that said the Administrative Judge ruled in my favor.

It was quite chaotic during the next three (3) weeks. There were calls and appointments for me and my initial MyoPro representative, Sarah Bui. She came and measured my right arm and hand. The MyoPro has to be manufactured to precise dimensions to the individual in order for it to function properly.

I had to wait for about three weeks for my MyoPro to be fabricated. Sarah Bui was the person who delivered it to my doorstep. She came in and instructed me how to control it. The fact of putting the MyoPro on my right arm and hand was quite a task. But now, I can do it (with the help of my wife, Paula) in less than a minute.

MyoMo Inc., the name of the entity that makes and distributes MyoPro, has two (2) different modes or approaches they are concerned with… 1) exercise and 2) function. Exercise is the different behaviors with your affected arm one can do in repetition. Function is the various movements one can do in and around your residence. Akin to lugging shopping bag from your car to the kitchen… opening a refrigerator door… picking a garden hose up from the lawn and so on and so forth.

I participated in a 12-month study where they took the various identical muscle movements and related them to the first month of the research. I assume I did quite well in my progression with the MyoPro but I never heard back of the corollaries.

It's been 56 years since my ischemic stroke. I was interested and immersed with the concept of doing things in and outside my residence without my MyoPro. I knew, realized and appreciated that working with the MyoPro was going to be a long endeavor.

SEE IN YOUR MIND'S EYE

Try to imagine or envision your life as a young adolescent. Walking and talking with humankind. A test in high school coming up Monday, a rehearsal that night in music or a 'heartthrob' was constantly on your mind. A sporting event that you were either going to participate in or be a supporter. And then suddenly… it all vanishes!?

It was a daunting task that lay ahead of me. My physical body was like day and night. The left side was fully functional.

All my muscles on my right side were paralyzed. Paralyzed means a condition in which voluntary muscle(s) are unable to move or act accordingly. It also denotes being powerless, inoperative or out of order.

I was totally forsaken of movement on my right side. My right-hand facial muscles were affected as well as my right shoulder, arm, hand, fingers, the upper and lower part of my leg, foot and finally the toes which we use in keeping balance. It even impacted the right side of my tongue.I couldn't communicate through verbal means. I could understand what was articulated and proclaimed to me. It was extremely difficult, challenging and incomprehensible to express my response and feelings. That's why I had such a taxing time expressing my way of thinking at the time.

I had aphasia and alexia. I couldn't read or interpret any written line like you're reading now or musical notes on a composition. I couldn't even write down the thoughts I was contemplating and considering on paper.

All these past subjects were things I did have and possess for the first 15 years of my life. That's why it was frustrating and dispiriting for me, personally, to come back. True, I could have just sat there and took it… teetered in a rocking chair for the rest of my life. But that proclamation said to me the night of the stroke kept reverberating in my mind whether subconsciously or consciously.

I had to do something. I had to try. After all, I was just a youngster… a young man trying to make a copious life for myself. I couldn't see living the rest of my life in this condition. And so many restrictions placed upon me I just had to break out to openness once more. Not being confined in 'this' limited and restrained status.

In a previous paragraph, I mentioned 'patience' when I was talking to the Administrative Court. You often hear that patience is a virtue. It's more than that. It involves and implies so many different attributes.

Basically, patience comes in two unique forms. First, success in various venues, and second, in the face of adversity, trial and/or delay. I exhibited both of these. Success in accomplishing the unthinkable. And adversity… coming back from a devastating stroke. The power to sit back and contemplate different situations and refashion the way to contest them. Patience is giving one the proficiency to calmly pause, enduring various burdens and knowing when to act and not to act.

Patience is the perspective concerning our desire and values in today's culture and society.

But one has to have that one unparalleled quality…perseverance. Perseverance entails the ability to learn from a problem or perplexity and try again.

I was talking to my neighbor, Dave Shaw (a highly religious individual) one day and said I would have to throw my pumpkins out because I didn't want them. In some fashion, over the winter the pumpkins crossbred with another vegetable species. The pumpkins came out with little bumps on the outside of the skin. He said, 'I'll come over and pick them up and feed them to my pigs.'

Accordingly, I was going through my pumpkin patch with Dave and weeding out all the unneeded pumpkins. One way or another, I briefly to him about my stroke scenario, and he said, 'What I would have done is collect Medicare from that day forward.' I looked up at him and said, 'I could have done that, but… I'm not made that way.'

It was quite silent through the rest of our harvesting. But I suppose my answer to Dave made him stop and wonder what kind of a neighbor he had.

For any culture or society to reach maturity one has to go through a formative interval. This stage is usually the 'teenage years!' He/she is in an adolescent podium which is going to make him/her into the person they will become or hope to become.

Most of all the young men and women are having fun, going to gatherings of some sort, attempting to prove their virility, independence and/or just out for a thing called mischief. It's a time when people experiment and try out different things in the psyche of adventure and gamble with this spectacle called life.

I never had any of that. I was trying to get back on my feet (literally) and struggling to cope with society. Mind you, society hadn't changed but I had! I was just determining a course that I could live and function with to make it through from day to day. I had different choices and consequences in my lifelong journey. And as one is reading this book… we all are doing it on a day-to-day basis!

The somebodies at home, at school whether it be the administrators, friends, family, teachers or students who knew what had happened to me were all attempting to be helpful. But they just didn't understand and comprehend the trauma and affliction that was going through my mind.

Every step I took, every movement I made, every utterance I spoke and every concept I distinguished and characterized had to be reworked and modified. I postulate this made me more uneasy and distraught than if they just left me alone. I was just attempting to get along with humanity.

However, this constant repetition and reiteration with the social order was actually an enticement, enhancement and encouragement to my normal self.

At the time, I thought I was being cheated and disillusioned through my teenage years. Why did He have to do this? Why me?

I see it now. He wanted to put me on a path that no one else could unravel and undertake. Just me. That's why He said, 'Jim… you can do better than that.'

It was a powerful declaration…

Life is a chance and adventure that nobody knows what it will entail.

The Lord knows… but that's the only One… Who does.